Praise for An Angel Treasury

'Jacky Newcomb has compiled probably the most fascinating
yet made available to the public. Filled with explanations of many of the most
frequently asked questions on angel phenomena, along with all the myth, facts
and theories, the book makes a brilliant read for anyone interested in Spirits
and the Host of Angels.'

COLIN FRY

**Star of LIVINGtv's *6ixth Sense with Colin Fry* and Director of the International
College of Spiritual Science and Healing, Ramsbergsgarden, Sweden**

'Everything you ever wanted to know about angels, and more!
Jacky and John Newcomb have compiled a unique guidebook to the angelic
realms. Informative, uplifting and heartwarming, no angel
lover should be without a copy.'

GLENNYCE ECKERSLEY

Author of *An Angel at my Shoulder*

'This truly is a treasury whether you are new to angel work, or work
regularly with these wondrous beings. It is filled with knowledge, compassion
and wisdom, but also a joy to read. As you read it you will know it is inspired
by angelic communication and will help even the most sceptical or diffident
reader to feel the brush of their wings.'

CASSANDRA EASON

Author, Broadcaster and Psychic Counsellor

'Jacky's book is inspirational, as well as a fascinating
source of information and wisdom.'

DIANA COOPER

Author of *A little Light on Angels*

'An Angel Treasury *brings the "other" world alive. If you don't believe in
angels, read Jacky Newcomb's compelling book – by the end you'll be utterly
convinced. I found it so gripping I stayed up all night and read it.'*

MARY BRYCE

Editor of *it's fate* magazine

'This is the only angel book I've read where there really doesn't seem to be a thing missing. I can't imagine a single question or fact about angels that isn't covered. How nice to have a book that doesn't just scratch the surface, but delves deep into the realm of angels, so that you come away not only with the sure certainty that angels are all around you, but an understanding of how they work and how to work with them. Jacky Newcomb's extensive knowledge is generously passed to the reader like drops of liquid gold. A true masterpiece!'

JENNY SMEDLEY
TV Presenter and Author of *Come Back to Life*

'Angels have always been part of my Qabala teaching, but until I read this book I was not aware of just how important they can be in my day-to-day living as well as those times when I am more in tune with less earthly visions – useful for those on a spiritual path and those about to make that first magical step.'

DAVID WELLS
TV Presenter, Astrologer and Medium, and Qabala Teacher

'If you have any questions about angels, you will find the answer here. In fact, you'll discover little gems about angels you never even thought to ask about! This is a book I will keep on my shelf forever and refer to over and over. It really is the ultimate book on angels.'

JILL WELLINGTON
Author of *Fireworks*, an American spiritual mystery

'As fast as mankind gains knowledge and awareness, at its expense, we are losing grasp of the intuitive ways of knowing. As Jacky Newcomb recounts, angels have touched our lives since man first inhabited the earth, and there certainly seems no signs of them relenting now!'

EMMA HEATHCOTE-JAMES
Author of *Seeing Angels* and *They Walk Among Us*

An Angel Treasury

An Angel Treasury

A Celestial Collection
of Inspirations, Encounters and Heavenly Lore

JACKY NEWCOMB
'The Angel Lady'

Additional research by John Newcomb

HarperElement
An Imprint of HarperCollins*Publishers*
77–85 Fulham Palace Road
Hammersmith, London W6 8JB

The website address is: www.thorsonselement.com

and *HarperElement* are registered trademarks of
HarperCollins*Publishers* Ltd

First published by HarperElement 2004

5 7 9 10 8 6

© Jacky Newcomb 2004

Jacky Newcomb asserts the moral right to
be identified as the author of this work

A catalogue record for this book
is available from the British Library

ISBN 0 00 718954 0

Printed and bound in Great Britain by
Martins The Printers, Berwick upon Tweed

Contents

Preface

In the last eight years, I have received letters from all over the world from people who want to know about angels and to share their own personal and private angel stories with me. Letters have come from all over the UK, and from America, Japan, Singapore, New Zealand, Australia, Canada and many European countries. All the letters and emails have arrived in response to my angel website, angel articles (in magazines such as *Lifted*, *Spiritual Lifestyles*, *Fate & Fortune*, *Prediction* and *Paradigm Shift*) and in my local newspaper, and my regular column, 'Dear Angel Lady' in *it's fate* magazine, as well as many articles on various websites around the world.

Readers' own letters, and the messages from my own angels in dreams and meditations, have been most influential in my communications with readers and visitors to my website. I soon discovered that people all over the world believe in angels. Angels are not restricted to any particular cultures or religions and, in fact, seem to be embraced by all.

The more people asked questions of 'The Angel Lady', the more I researched. The more I discovered about angels, I realized the less I actually knew about them. In fact, the less *any* of us know about them! Type in the word 'Angel' or 'Archangel' into any Internet search engine and you will pull up as many as 100,000 websites – all devoted to angels and angel experiences. Thousands of personal websites are decorated with angel images and share angel stories, angel quotes and angel references. Angels are as big now – or even bigger – than they were in biblical times and the age of the Renaissance painters. Angels are *hot*! Rest assured, I don't mean that in any disrespectful way! We are rediscovering angels in new and exciting ways.

Angels have become a part of the clothing we wear, decorating everything from hats to T-shirts. You find their images on mugs, pictures, magazines and books, stickers, jewellery, posters, postcards, cosmetics, bags and even hot-water bottle covers! Many people have angel figurines around their homes or wear a guardian angel pin on their jackets and coats. Other people carry around a guardian angel coin or token as a sign that they believe and want to be protected by these angel guardians.

People are no longer embarrassed to talk about their hopes and fears surrounding angels. Even the strongest and most macho of men will share their own angel experiences after a drink or two at the local bar (usually whispered, when their friends aren't listening!) … at least, they happily share their stories with me!

The smallest of children have witnessed these celestial beings – many before they are even aware of what an 'angel' is or means. People who are ill or in difficulties, emotionally and physically, have born witness to the angels.

Angels are real!

After a while, I realized that many people wanted to know the answers to the same questions over and over again. I would receive the same queries every single week. This is where the idea for my first angel book came from. Everything you always wanted to know about angels – and more.

No one is a real angel expert. No one will know everything about angels until we meet with them again in the after-life – but we do know a lot about them. I want to share the knowledge that I've learnt about angels and how they help us and work with us in our lives. I hope you enjoy using this book as much as I have enjoyed creating it for you.

Jacky Newcomb

Acknowledgements

*W*riting a book takes time and energy. My husband John spent many hours researching, typing and proof reading. My daughters Charlotte and Georgina had to make their own dinner – a lot! Bless you for your patience. And to my Mum and Dad, who've believed in me always.

There are many editors who have supported me in my writing career, including Mary Bryce and Tania Ahsan. I thank them all.

I want to acknowledge also my sisters Debbie, Dilly and Di, and my lovely friends Wendy, Maria and Sally who helped to keep my feet on the ground.

To my many Angel Lady friends, especially Diana Cooper, Glennyce Eckersley and Emma Heathcote-James; I thank you for your inspiration. To my friend Martine Angéle, who shows me different ways of looking at angels. To my dear friend David Wells, who makes me laugh when the going gets tough, and Colin Fry, for your support and friendship.

But most of all I want to thank my friend, the author Jill Wellington, who has held my hand every step of the way, read my articles and notes, helped to guide me and even helped to source angel stories along the way. I could never have done it without you.

About the Author

*J*acky Newcomb is one of the UK's leading paranormal writers and angel experts.

Her work features in the UK's foremost paranormal and mystical magazines *it's fate*, *Prediction*, and *Fate & Fortune magazine*. In addition, she has produced features and articles for many non-paranormal women's magazines in the UK and around the world (including *Chat* and *Woman's Own*) as well as for many newspapers and website features.

She runs her own 'mystical agony aunt' column, 'Dear Angel Lady', for *it's fate* magazine, which draws queries about paranormal experiences from all over the country.

Jacky has collected angel stories from around the world. She writes regularly about angels, spirit guides and after-life communication, and has appeared on television programmes such as Granada TV's *This Morning* and LIVINGtv's *Psychic Live*.

Jacky lives in a small village in the UK with her husband and co-researcher John. They have two children. Jacky and John run their own company, *Gabriel Media*, through which they run an on-line shop and regularly host workshops on a variety of spiritual subjects, including angels.

Jacky can be contacted via her website: http://www.angellady.co.uk

1

Frequently Asked Questions

and

Angel Quotes

Frequently Asked Questions and Angel Quotes

'We are like children, who stand in need of masters to enlighten us and direct us, and God has provided for this by appointing his angels to be our teachers and guides.'

SAINT THOMAS AQUINAS

I receive hundreds of emails to my website and from my magazine and newspaper column about angels. Many people are interested in their own angels in particular. But many more people just want to know what an angel is and what an angel isn't!

Here are some of the most frequently asked angel questions I have received, and some of the more unusual ones.

There are also hundreds of fascinating angel quotes, some which reference questions here, so I have included some of them too.

What is an angel?

A short question with a long answer but I will try to be brief. Angels were made by our God essence or energy. The role of angels is varied but many angels have been created specifically with the purpose of looking after God's children – us.

'An angel is a spiritual being created by God, without a body,
for the service of Christendom and the Church.'

MARTIN LUTHER *TABLE TALK*

Can my Grandma be my Angel?

Human spirits cannot be our angels insomuch as an angel can never be human and a human can never be an angel (with the exception of the Archangels Metatron and Sandalphon – *see* 'Archangels', page 147). Most traditions say that humans can never be angels. Having said that, the loving spirits of passed-over relatives can and do watch over us from the other-side. They are able to send us loving energy in a similar way to angels.

Humans are spirit in the body-vessel, but angels are pure light energy.

'The angels are a strange genus; they are precisely what they are
and cannot be anything else. They are themselves soulless beings who
represent nothing but the thoughts and intuitions of their Lord.'

C. G. JUNG

Many people see their relatives visit them from 'the other-side' where they appear in a body-less form, often surrounded by a white light. This is where the confusion may arise. Our loved ones can watch out for us and often make it their specific task to act as our 'guardians' by passing us messages of warnings and so on. There are vast numbers of recorded incidences where the loving spirits of our relatives who have gone before, appear to 'guide and protect' from the after-life.

Shona wrote to tell me about her own experience:

'When I was 14 my grandma passed to spirit and I was devastated because we were really close! About two weeks later I could not sleep and felt guided down the stairs to the kitchen. No lights were on and there were no windows from which a light could have shone from outside! Yet there was the most brilliant white light over the boiler, and it was full of peace and calm. I felt drawn towards it and just stood with this energy. It made me feel so serene just like my Nan always had! I know it was her!

When my mother-in-law passed to spirit, it was a very stressful time for my husband. His Dad, who was left behind, lives in Bournemouth and we live in London, which is a big distance away!

We went up to visit once a month. The first time we went the energy was so cold and deadly! The next time I called to my mother-in-law Dorothy to tell her I was really stressed and needed to know she would help, and when we arrived at the flat it felt warm and lived in! My husband always multi-checks everything before leaving a house so I know all appliances had been switched off!

I know if you ask, spirit will come but just not always as you expect. Often lights flicker, TVs turn on and off, and things get moved, but I say "God bless" each time, knowing my loved ones are always close!'

Are angels like ghosts?

Not at all, and this is a common confusion. Ghosts are the 'lost souls of the dead', or 'spirits in visitation', from the 'other-side'. The confusion with angel guardians arose with the birth of Spiritualism, and the belief that the spirit of our loved ones are 'watching us' from the after-life.

Angels just 'are', and are beings without spirit at all, who exist in the realms of heaven.

How can an angel help me?

Angels do not have a full understanding of what it is to be human, so they do not always understand our problems totally. Angels are good at placing the right people into our path when we need them (set up as a useful 'coincidence' for the purpose of guidance and moving us forward with our pre-birth life plans), and specifically at sending us loving energy and support.

Angels do have speciality roles and we can call upon a specific angel to help with certain tasks (*see* the Angel Almanac, page 33, for a detailed list).

> *'When you are lonely or frightened, talk to your guardian angel.*
> *You can do it out loud or inside your head – your angel can hear you.*
> *Ask your angel to be near you, to put his or her hand on your*
> *shoulder to give you courage and protect you.'*
>
> JOAN WESTER ANDERSON *WHERE ANGELS WALK*

Angels are very good at bringing the right information to our attention and placing the right people into our path.

*'Friends are angels who lift us to our feet when our
wings have trouble remembering how to fly.'*

ANONYMOUS

*If we have angels around us, why is it that
things go wrong in our lives?*

As spirit we move into a human body to work through lessons and goals that
we set for ourselves before birth. (We pre-plan skills that we need to practise.)
Angels are not allowed to interfere with this plan (or they would be meddling
with our curriculum).

Sometimes these lessons are much harder than we ever imagined they
might be and this is how an angel can help. They can ease a difficult situation
and help us through the pain. They can bring along sympathetic people to help
us achieve our goals and support us in times of difficulty. There is one important
proviso: we have to ask our angels for their assistance. They need our permission
to get involved in our lives. Of course, emergencies are different!

'Angels do find us in our hour of need.'

AMY HUFFMAN

How can I give my angels permission to help me?

Nothing complicated is needed here – just ask! You can ask by talking to your angels out loud, or you can ask in your head, write them a letter or use some other symbol of request. Nowadays it is easy to find those little 'guardian angel pins' or tokens and coins with the words 'guardian angel' printed on them. All of these act as requests for help. Every time we look at these little symbols we think of our angels and this strengthens the contact.

'You don't need a formal prayer or invocation to call the Angels to your side. Simply think, Angels, please surround me, and they are there.'

DOREEN VIRTUE, *DIVINE GUIDANCE*

If you like to be a little more creative in your approach, then the section on Communicating With Your Angels (page 281) may help you.

What can I do to thank my angel?

Prayer is very powerful indeed (in whatever form feels right for you), or you can just say a normal 'thank you' in the same way that you would thank any friend:

'...angels, I would like to thank you for your assistance and support in my life and would like to invite you to continue to be at my side for all time...'

The angels' greatest wish is that we love one another. There is no greater gift to the angels. Try practising random acts of kindness. Pass on loving energy to another human being.

*'And the Angel said, "I have learned that every man lives,
not through care of himself, but by love."'*

LEO TOLSTOY

What is the purpose of the angel statues, pictures and things with angels on them?

Angels appear in many different forms, but believe it or not, it does not matter to the angels how they appear in our symbolism of them. They are very attracted to the energy that surrounds anything which we use as a representation of an angel. The angels understand our intent and that is what is important.

If the angel item is attractive to you then it will contain your own loving energy and meaning. Whatever item you buy or make is perfect for you. Many people feel that these images contain power in themselves, and I certainly believe that objects can hold energy imprints. Remember that these objects can act as a reminder of the angels' love for us, but we do not 'need' them in order to work with angels or have their presence around us.

Is it true that we all have our own guardian angel with us all the time?

It is my understanding that we all have spiritual guides of some sort with us all of the time. Our guides act as teachers and friends on the other-side but with the knowledge and experience of being human that angels do not possess.

'For every soul, there is a guardian watching it.'

THE KORAN

Some people (depending on our task and roles in life) have many angels with them all the time, and others have angels with them only when they are needed (or called for by ourselves or our guides). We can call upon angels at any time if we feel we need help, guidance or protection. Use any words that feel appropriate to you, and remember to say thank you after your request.

'...I would like to ask for the assistance/protection of angel [add angel name here] right now. I thank you for any help you are able to give me...'

What do angels look like?

Angels often appear in a way in which we expect to see them. Some people see angels as sparks or clouds of light or energy; some people see a traditional 'Christmas Card' angel, complete with wings and halos, and yet others see them more in human form. They can appear as very small figures or very large, tall and imposing visions – with their heads through the ceiling and their 'feet' through the floor!

Usually visitations appear either in one's 'mind's eye' or just with a 'knowing that they are there'. Angels can be sensed and heard, as well as seen.

How do we know what angels look like?

Well that's a good question! Recordings of angel sightings appear as far back as documented text! We have literally thousands of descriptions of angels. There are many incidences of angel appearances in religious documents like the Bible and the Koran and even today, hundreds of people see and sense angels during times of stress and great need. Angels appear in such writings as the Books of Enoch, and their descriptions are very different to our current portrayals of them.

Some angels stand as tall as the heavens; Archangel Metatron is covered with 365,000 eyes and 36 pairs of wings, and created as pure flame! When they visit the earth realm angels take on a different appearance and can show themselves to us in any way they wish.

What is angel music?

People often try to re-create the 'sounds of the spheres' (the musical sounds created by angels). The area in 'heaven' that produces the unbelievable angel music is believed to be over England – although people all over the world do hear angel music.

Individuals lucky enough to hear 'celestial sounds' (orchestral harmonies produced as a communication of joy by the angels) say that it sounds like nothing that they have ever heard before. People hear angel music in answer to a request for healing, at times of danger, during moments of great joy and when loved ones are crossing over to the other-side. Sometimes this momentous and wondrous harmony is heard for no apparent reason at all!

I have been blessed to hear this music myself – something I will remember for the rest of my life.

'Music is well said to be the speech of angels.'

THOMAS CARLYLE

There are also angels, called Herald Angels, whose specific job is to trumpet messages and announcements. The most famous instance of this was the moment the herald of angels came to proclaim the birth of Jesus Christ.

Bene Elim (meaning 'sons of God') are angels or archangels who sing the praises of God.

When you see an angel do you always hear music?

No. Some people hear music, some hear bells or 'human-like' voices. Others hear nothing at all.

'Every time you hear a bell ring, it means that some angel's just got his wings.'

HENRY TRAVERS TO JIMMY STEWART IN
IT'S A WONDERFUL LIFE.

Would angels be looking after my son who died as a small baby?

Angels are regularly seen by the dying and those sitting with the dying. They appear to help our loved ones cross over to the other-side and support and care for them when they get there. For more details see the specific references to Archangel Azrael, who traditionally has been called 'angel of death'. Nowadays we would probably call them the 'passing-over' angels.

Is it true that children can see angels when adults can't?

Sometimes this does seem to be the case. I think that with younger children, especially, it is because they do not know that others can't! The other explanations that adults look for to explain visions simply do not occur to a child! They go for the most obvious explanation – if it looks like an angel then it is one!

> *'Perhaps children's innocence, wherever it comes from, contributes to the fact that they seem to see angels more often.'*
>
> JOHN RONNER, *KNOW YOUR ANGELS*

Some stories reach me where very small children describe or talk to an angel when their parents say that they have no prior knowledge of what an angel might be! Although in most nursery and junior schools (at least in the UK) even the very tiniest of children take part in nativity plays and dress up as angels!

What's the difference between an angel and an archangel?

The word 'angel' is the collective name for all the 'celestial beings'. There is an 'angelic hierarchy' of angels, with angels divided between three spheres. In the group of angels closest to earth (the third sphere) and working with humankind are the angels we usually call 'Guardian Angels'.

In many references the archangels are said to be the higher-ranking angels.

Do all angels have wings?

Many religious sources do list certain angels as having wings. The Archangel Gabriel is said to have 140 wings! Some people see angels with wings and some do not. Many people believe that angels are beings of light and do not need wings at all, and that it's the 'light' which is mistaken for wings. This idea is thought to go back to the earliest times when humankind assumed that to fly, an angel would need such assistance.

Some people who see angels believe that the 'wings' are, in fact, streams of upward-flowing energy.

Winged creatures were known to the Vikings, who called them 'valkyries'; the Greeks called them the 'horae'. The Greek god Hermes served as a messenger and was shown with wings on his feet. Do these early references contribute to the angels-have-wings tradition? Angels were not really known as having wings (with any regularity at least) until the time of the Emperor Constantine in the fourth century after Christ, and it is the art of the Renaissance which gives us much of our angel imagery. In the Bible, for example, the angels who gave the news of the resurrection of Jesus are described as 'two men', but they appear in the light associated with angels.

Ancient cave drawings and carvings do show beings with wings. Were these angels or something else? We may never know.

Do all angels visit the earth?

No, I don't believe they do, although many angels are assigned the role of guardians of the Earth and protectors of humans. Many millions more have roles in heaven and other realms and planes of existence.

Sometimes angels are known to pass their message through people rather than enter our atmosphere, which is difficult for them to do. It can also be frightening for humans!

Do angels go to other planets?

Almost certainly. Each planet has its own angels who look over it.

Have angels existed since the beginning of time?

Yes, angels were made right at the beginning and the spirit that resides in the human form was made later, but as to whether angels were created just before or just after the beginning of the world is up for debate.

'On the second day, God created the angels with their natural propensity to good. Later He made beasts with their animal desires. But God was pleased with neither. So He fashioned man, a combination of angel and beast, free to follow good or evil.'

HEBREW BIBLICAL TEXT

In Psalm 148 in the old Testament it says,

'Praise the Lord from the heavens, praise him in the heights! Praise him all his angels praise him, all his host! ... Let them praise the name of the Lord! For he commanded and they were created.'

Others believe that the seven great archangels were made to help with the building of the Cosmos. Jewish writings suggest that they came into existence each morning through the breath of God, only to be reabsorbed each evening after their work had been completed. The Catholic Church teaches that before

God made the world he made the angels – and all in one go! So I guess the answer to that question depends on whom you ask.

How many angels are there?

Many times it is quoted that there are more angels in the heavens than there are men on the Earth which will put the numbers of angels at billions!
    Jesus said:

> *'Do you think I cannot call my Father, and he will at once put at my disposal more than twelve legions of angels?'*
>
> MATTHEW 26:53

There is also another mention in the Bible:

> *'Then I looked and heard the voice of many angels numbering thousands upon thousands, and ten thousand times ten thousand.'*
>
> BIBLE, REV 5:1

Are angels common to all religions?

Yes, most religions recognize angels in one form or another. Not all religions call them angels, but they do recognize wise and loving beings of light who work with us from another plane of existence. The Hindus, for example, have devas ('the shining ones') who do a similar work to angels, and the Buddhist equivalent of an angel is also a diva, with their form described as spiritual beings with light emanations. They are recognized as enlightened beings. In Judaism, the 'malachim' are messengers of God.

Do angels have halos?

The halo appeared in the fourth century as an artistic development! In biblical times, angels were seen (or at least reported) on a more regular basis. Angels, as beings of pure light, are surrounded by a glow. This aura of light is what is believed to have been interpreted as a 'halo' in all the great renaissance angel paintings. So angels do not just have halos, they are halos!

Do angels have relationships or partners?

Angels do not have relationships in the way that we would understand. Their role is one of pure love and service to the divine. So their relationships are with God, rather than as we would think of relationships.

Jesus was asked if a person had been married more than once, whom would they be with at the resurrection. Jesus explained that,

> *'At the resurrection, men and women do not marry; they are like the angels in heaven.'*
>
> MATTHEW 22:30

Which would indicate this fact that relationships are not part of an angels specification.

Are angels male or female?

Angels are actually androgynous (having no sex), but are sometimes shown (or show themselves) as male or female to indicate traditional masculine or feminine tendencies such as gentleness or strength. The Bible for example shows Gabriel to be a female but the Moslems recognize a male Gabriel, 'Jibril', who dictated the Koran to the prophet Mohammed.

Increasingly, I believe that this is unnecessary and angels will more and more show themselves with no sex. As we soften and merge the lines between the sexes, so the angels will take their clue from us.

Do angels eat?

There are many stories where angels have appeared as human and have pretended to eat in order to make us feel more comfortable, but they live on 'the love of god' and food as we know and understand it is not required for sustenance. There are references to angels and food however. Jesus was brought food and water by a helpful angel when he spent his forty days in the wilderness.

'Manna' is said to be the food of the angels – food given as a gift from the angels. Mann is a Hebrew word and translates as 'what is this?' The Israelites (during the Exodus) thought that they might starve to death, but God promised them food: *'...there in the wilderness, fine flakes appeared, fine as hoar-frost on the ground. When the Israelites saw it, they said to one another, "What is it?" because they did not know what it was. Moses said to them, "That is the bread which the Lord has given you to eat..."'* (Exodus 16:13-15).

Metatron is the angel in charge of human sustenance.

Do all angels have names?

No, and they do not recognize the need for names at all. Angels are distinguished for their abilities and roles, and it is only the human need to name things which is the reason they have attracted names as we know and understand them.

'Angels are spirits, but it is not because they are spirits that they are angels. They become angels when they are sent, for the name angel refers to their office, not their nature. You may ask the name of this nature, it is spirit; you ask its office, it is that of an angel, which is a messenger.'

SAINT AUGUSTINE

How do I find out the name of my angel?

Angels have no problem with us using names, however, and are just happy to be noticed and utilized. We can call our angels anything at all – whatever feels right for us. If you prefer, you can ask for a name in meditation or just before going to sleep at night. Take the first name that comes to you.

If angels exist, why can't we see them more often?

Angels' roles are to work 'behind the scenes'. Our dense atmosphere on the earth plane makes it difficult for them to manifest physically for any length of time – although they do make appearances occasionally in subtle ways.

Angels also appear in dreams, and sometimes when we are 'crossing over' or during near-death experiences. It is during these times when our own consciousness has moved away from the earth plane (when we are asleep or unconscious) that angels can appear to us physically.

The sudden visual appearance might frighten most of us, I'm sure. If you take a look at the majority of angel appearances in the Bible, those who came in contact with the celestial being were struck with terror!

'The guardian Angels of life sometimes fly so high as to be
beyond our sight, but they are always looking down upon us.'

JEAN PAUL RICHTER

Why do some people see colours when they see angels?

Angels produce colour as part of their energy field, as beings of 'white light'. White of course splits into all the colours of the rainbow. During near-death experiences, when people feel themselves leave the physical body, they sometimes see colours that do not exist on the physical plane (our sphere of existence).

The colours that each angel shows make up part of their personality. Colour is also connected to sound and is an indication of a sound frequency.

Can we ask for angels to help others?

Yes we can, although our call will only be answered if it is for the highest good of that person, or with the consent of that person's higher spirit or higher self.

Angels long to be called into service, so it is always worth asking for help on behalf of another person, with the proviso '…with the will of God and the highest possible outcome for the progression of the spirit [of the individual concerned]'. Don't worry if you forget. As long as your intention is pure!

Many believe that the angels have more power to help if we invite them to do so. Asking for help isn't going to hurt anyway!

Are they extra-dimensional or extra-terrestrial beings?

Angels are not extra-terrestrial insomuch as they do not 'live' on other planets. It would be more correct to call them 'inter-dimensional beings', as they move between worlds or spiritual planes.

Are they eternal?

With God's will, yes.

Do they age?

Not in the way that we would age, no. As angels do not have bodies, and passage of time has no meaning in heaven, age is of no relevance.

Are they still being formed? (Is Michael older than other angels?)

The angels were created at different times, or not, depending on which source you read! Gabriel, Michael, Raphael and Uriel (or Ariel) are usually said to have been formed at the same time, though. Are angels still being formed? I think that only God knows the answer to that one, but spirit is being created continuously so I don't see why not.

Are the 'Fab Four' (Michael, Gabriel, Uriel, Raphael) the strongest, or just the most popular?

Michael and Gabriel are given 'leader titles' in many texts. They are the most well known of angels, which may make them seem the most popular. Michael, Gabriel, Uriel and Raphael are also thought to have guardianship over the Earth and so are 'our' angels.

Can people become angels, or just saints?

Angels have been named saints, but people are not made into angels (in most traditions). Having said that, there are two archangels who are said to be the ascended spirits of humans: Archangel Metatron was given the role of an angel (having once walked the earth as Enoch) for his services to God whilst in human form. Other sources say that the Archangel Sandalphon (recognized as the twin of Archangel Metatron) was once the prophet Elijah.

These two are certainly exceptions to the rule, because the spirit that resides in the human body is of a different form and type to that which is angel.

'Every man contemplates an angel in his future self.'

RALPH WALDO EMERSON

'I have been on the verge of being an angel all my life, but it's never happened yet.'

MARK TWAIN

The Mormons recognize the angel Moroni, who visited their founding prophet Joseph Smith. Moroni was said to be once human and the son of the prophet Mornon, and to have become an angel after his death, and there is a statue of Moroni on top of most Mormon temples.

Kabbalists (followers of a Jewish mystical tradition) also believe that as well as being created by God special humans can also develop into angels.

Have angels ever incarnated?

As far as we know, only Enoch and Elijah have ever been human, although angels do make brief appearances in human form.

'Be not forgetful to entertain strangers, for therby some have entertained angels unawares.'

HEBREWS 13:2

How would I be able to contact angels?

In any number of simple ways beginning with 'just ask them'. For more ideas, check out the section on Communicating With Your Angels, page 281.

'We should pray to the angels, for they are given to us as guardians.'

ST AMBROSE

What do our angels actually do for us?

They send us positive thoughts and energy, and love and protection (in its simplest form).

'What know we of the Blest above but that they sing, and that they love?'

WILLIAM WORDSWORTH

How much are they permitted to do to help us?

They are not allowed to interfere with our 'free will' or anything that may obstruct with any lessons we have pre-planned for ourselves. Although angels do help to lessen the pain, or help with variations of a plan when a choice is proving too difficult for us. Sometimes our pre-birth choices are just too hard for us to handle!

'We are never so lost our angels cannot find us.'

STEPHANIE POWERS

I often see people in my room at night. Are they angels or are they spirits who want to communicate with me?

Probably spirits. But they may not want to communicate, see you, or even know that you can see them. Spirit overlays our very life – heaven is not 'up there' but right here. During the night our own spirit is more fluid within our bodily shell which takes us closer to the realms of spirit (we sort of meet 'in the middle'). You can ask your angels to help make these spirits unseen to you if this is what you want.

*'Goodnight, sweet prince, and flights of angels
sing thee to thy rest.'*

WILLIAM SHAKESPEARE *HAMLET*, ACT V, SCENE 2

How do I know if my angel is with me?
What signs of their presence should I look for?

Angels are around us a lot but if you want further proof of their presence you can always ask them for a sign. Don't expect a being of light to suddenly jump out of the wardrobe – it simply doesn't work that way. They will indicate they are around in more subtle ways.

Sometimes they will communicate their message through a stranger. A woman at the bus stop may strike up a 'meaningful' conversation for example. Someone may present you with an angel pin, or perhaps a white feather will appear where there were none before. Maybe you will just 'feel' your angel come close to you.

'All God's angels come to us disguised.'

JAMES RUSSELL LOWELL

How do our angels choose us?

Angels are attracted to our energy and goals … like a magnet!

Do we choose our own angels between lives?

It doesn't really work like that with angels. We each have spirit guides (more advanced and experienced souls like ourselves) whom we plan to work with during our life on earth.

Are angels similar to the spirit guides that mediums use or are they not permitted to perform this function?

No, not really, although mediums can communicate with angels in this way, they usually don't.

Are they the messengers of God as the Bible claimed, or do they have a different purpose?

One of the translations of Angel is 'Messenger' but they have so many more roles!

*'Beside each man who's born on earth, a guardian angel takes
his stand, to guide him through life's mysteries.'*

MENANDER OF ATHENS

Does helping us help them? (In other words, by helping us in our lives are they paying back a karmic debt in their own?)

No. Angels are created as pure beings of light and are not thought to follow the same rules of Karma as ourselves. Helping us brings them extreme joy. It is their very reason for being.

After their present ward's life has ended, do they become 'assigned' to another soul or is their task completed?

Life for the angels continues much as before. Angels are able to be in many places at one time (not being governed by our own laws of space and time), and so are helping many people at any one time.

> *'Our Lord is God [alone], and wholeheartedly pursue the right way –*
> *upon them do angels descend, saying "fear not and grieve not, but*
> *receive the good news … we are your supporters in the present life*
> *and in the life to come." '*
>
> THE KORAN

Is it true that white feathers are a sign that your angel is near?

Many people believe so. Feathers are free, lightweight and available in most places around the world – which makes them the perfect physical manifestation. Many people associate white feathers with the 'wings' of an angel.

When I appeared on Granada TV's *This Morning* I answered listeners questions on angels and 'feathers' was a topic which came up with several callers and we had a lot of fun in the studio. It's a question that I also get asked about regularly in my 'Dear Angel Lady' column with *it's fate* magazine.

Elaine emailed me and asked why she was having so many problems in her life. She found it hard to believe that she had angels around her, although she did feel that maybe she had been led to write to me in some way.

After reading my reply and giving it some thought, she decided to invite angels into her life. On the first day nothing happened, which confirmed, she said, her belief that they had turned their backs on her. She decided to ask them for a sign like a feather as I had suggested, to let her know they were with her.

The next day, Elaine was in the supermarket shopping with her young family. In her own words, she was busy and hassled with the four kids and packing her shopping when she opened up a half packed bag to put in some more shopping. Guess what she found? A feather! She told me it was just laying there, a pink feather of the sort you might find in a feather boa. She couldn't believe it and said there was no way it could have come from the children or been in the bag to start with. Elaine firmly believes that this was a sign that they are with her!

It was fun to receive her follow-up letter and her big 'thank you'. But it was her own angels – and I cannot take the credit. The story was another gift of confirmation for me that our angels really are around us.

Can they prevent us from harm? Do they ever try to prevent our deaths?

It seems that they can and do protect people from death and serious accident if it is not part of a person's life-lessons (the lessons we choose for ourselves before birth). I have received letters from all over the world where people have seen their angels, or an angel has intervened during a near-death experience.

'He shall give his angels charge over thee,
to keep thee in all thy ways.'

PSALM 9:11

Are angels around children when they are born, (those with difficult births?)

Certainly. Our angels are always around us during times of difficulty offering healing and support.

Do you think there is any truth to the idea that ancients mistook visitors from other planets as angels?

This is something we just don't know but cave paintings include images which look a little like a cross between angels and our present-day astronauts – so you never know!

Are angels just energy?

Angels are made of light and love. Their bodies do not exist as solid flesh in our dimension. They have no need of clothes – but appear draped in cloth sometimes (for our own modesty). They do not speak with words as we would speak but transmit thought and feelings as a kind of telepathy.

'Angels are intelligent reflections of light, that original light which has no beginning. They can illuminate. They do not need tongues or ears, for they can communicate without speech, in thought.'

JOHN OF DAMASCUS

2

Angel Almanac

Angel Almanac

The archangels each have their own specialities, talents and roles, although not everyone agrees on what these might be! Some of these roles are traditional and some are more modern interpretations of the archangels' own skill areas. Each of these angels has their own area of expertise and many people wish to work with the right angel for the right job! You probably wouldn't call a plumber to lay your carpets or expect a beautician to be the best person to fix your car, so this makes a lot of sense.

Some of the archangels' roles are more obvious. For example, Raphael is the patron of doctors and therapists (one of the translations of his name is 'Divine Healer'). Gabriel is well known as a messenger angel, so naturally Gabriel is the patron of messengers and postal workers. This stems back from 1951 when Pope Pius XII declared Gabriel to be the angel over all areas of telecommunications!

ANGELS OF ASSISTANCE

Do be assured though that the plumber might actually know a carpet-fitter, even if he can't do the job personally. So if in doubt, ask. Just call on 'the best angel for the job'. Imagine your own spirit guides like a directories service – the right angel will be found, even if you don't know the number. You could call on the angels like this:

> **'...beloved guides, I ask for your assistance in finding an angel expert in finding lost keys/unblocking my drains/ to help me with my schoolwork etc...'**

Archangel Michael is well known as an angel who can help with mechanical things. Teresa asked him for help directly, with the back up of other angels, and emailed me to tell me what happened:

> *Recently I found myself in dire straits and needed to sell my car. I had been let down by a few buyers (and it had been on the market for some months). I needed the money to deposit in the bank this very same day so that I could pay my mortgage later that week. There was another problem – the car tax had expired and so I could not drive the car anywhere. I needed not only someone to buy the car, but to also come and pick it up with a truck.*
>
> *I thought this impossible and so I decided to pray to my Angels for a miracle. I would like to add that up until this day I had been waking up each night at 2:22 a.m. and felt this was somehow relevant, a message from the Angels. I prayed very hard to Archangel Michael and made a shrine dedicated to the Angels, and placed the cards of Archangel Michael, Archangel Uriel and Archangel Gabriel on the shrine along with a fresh purple flower from my garden. I also placed two purple candles, which I lit in honour of the Angels.*

Approximately 22 minutes later my phone rang and I dashed to pick up the call only to find a garage some 65 miles away that had seen my car for sale and wanted to purchase it, but alas they could not pick it up so my hopes were dashed. As soon as I put the phone down it rang instantly and I picked it right up, to discover it was another local garage offering to buy my car that very day – and said they could pick my car up and also write me a cheque to deposit in my bank that day.

I was shocked needless to say, but also in awe of my Angels, they really did save me that day!'

ANGELIC HELP WITH LIFE'S PROBLEMS

If you're the sort of person that likes to 'dial direct,' then this table may help you.

SPECIFIC LIFE PROBLEM	ARCHANGEL HELPER
Arguments, disagreements, unresolved problems, legal wrangles	Ariel, Raguel and Gabriel
Childbirth, childcare, pregnancy and adoptions	Gabriel, Raphael and Sandalphon
Communications, letter writing, telephone calls, emails	Gabriel and Metatron
Creativity, making things, designing	Gabriel and Jophiel
Development problems, slow progress	Raphael
Fixing/mending broken items and problems	Michael
Gardening, farming, landscaping, earth healing, plants and flowers	Uriel
Grief, dying, and serious illness counselling, and care of the dying and bereaved	Azrael and Raphael

SPECIFIC LIFE PROBLEM	ARCHANGEL HELPER
Healing, health, operations, medical issues	Metatron and Raphael
Homes, living accommodation	Chamuel
Lack of confidence, personal issues, tears	Zadkiel and Sandalphon
Learning, studying, exams, interviews and speeches	Haniel and Uriel
Lost objects, missing items	Chamuel
Mathematical problems	Raziel
Money worries, financial security	Michael
Pet care, healing and health of animals and birds	Ariel
Protection, safety, security,	Chamuel
Psychic development, clairvoyance	Jeremiel
Remembering things, memory	Zadkiel
Romantic love and personal relationships	Haniel
Sleeping problems	Michael
Spiritual development, faith	Metatron and Sandalphon
Travelling, transport	Raphael
World events, world peace	Chamuel

ANGELS AND HOBBIES

Angels look over all sorts of pursuits. Archangel Gabriel works with all creative endeavours and is mentioned in all hobbies and pastimes on the list below (which is by no means comprehensive!). The more complicated the hobby, the more angels have an interest; activities which involve other people also have the interests of several angels.

Each archangel is responsible for different aspects of the activity. For example fishing involves a variety of angel gifts (patience, water, fish, etc.), with each area having different archangels in charge. To work on these activities, call on any, or all of the archangels listed. If you want to pick one, go with your first instinct – you have your own ability to know which archangel is the right one to call.

Hobbies, Interests and Pastimes	*Archangel*
Aerobics	Gabriel, Metatron
Aircraft Spotting	Gabriel, Metatron
Alternative Health	Gabriel, Raphael, Raziel, Sariel, Uriel, Zadkiel
Amateur Astronomy	Gabriel, Raziel
Amateur Radio	Gabriel, Haniel, Michael
Angling	Ariel, Azriel, Gabriel, Haniel, Michael, Raphael
Animals	Ariel, Gabriel, Michael, Raphael

HOBBIES, INTERESTS AND PASTIMES	ARCHANGEL
Antiques	Gabriel, Michael
Arts and Crafts	Azriel, Gabriel, Haniel, Jophiel, Uriel
Artwork	Azriel, Gabriel, Jophiel, Uriel
Autographs	Gabriel, Haniel
Autosport	Gabriel, Metatron
Backgammon	Gabriel, Michael
Baseball Cards	Gabriel, Haniel
Baseball, Softball and Rounders	Gabriel, Metatron
Bike	Gabriel, Metatron
Bird Feeding	Ariel, Gabriel, Jeremiel, Metatron, Zadkiel
Bird Watching	Ariel, Gabriel, Haniel, Metatron, Raphael, Zadkiel
Board Games	Gabriel, Michael
Boating	Gabriel, Metatron
Books	Gabriel, Sariel
Bowling	Gabriel
Bridge	Gabriel, Michael
Bus Spotting	Gabriel, Metatron, Raguel
Butterfly Watching	Ariel, Gabriel, Haniel, Raphael, Zadkiel
Campaigning	Gabriel, Haniel, Jeremiel, Jophiel, Michael, Raguel

Hobbies, Interests and Pastimes	Archangel
Canoeing	Ariel, Gabriel, Metatron
Card Games	Gabriel, Haniel, Michael, Uriel
Cars	Gabriel
Caving	Gabriel, Metatron
Chess	Gabriel, Haniel, Michael, Uriel
Cinema	Gabriel
Classic Bikes	Gabriel, Michael
Classic Cars	Gabriel, Jophiel, Michael
Clubs	Gabriel, Metatron, Raguel, Uriel
Coins	Gabriel, Raguel
Collecting	Gabriel, Raguel
Comic Books	Gabriel, Raguel
Company	Gabriel, Haniel, Raguel, Zadkiel
Computer Games	Gabriel, Michael
Computer Programming	Gabriel, Haniel, Jophiel
Concerts	Gabriel, Haniel, Raguel, Sandalphon
Cooking	Azriel, Gabriel, Jophiel, Raguel
Countryside	Gabriel, Metatron
Crafts	Azriel, Gabriel, Haniel, Jophiel, Uriel
Crochet	Azriel, Gabriel, Jophiel, Uriel
Cross Stitch	Azriel, Gabriel, Jophiel, Uriel

HOBBIES, INTERESTS AND PASTIMES	ARCHANGEL
Crosswords	Chamuel, Gabriel, Uriel
Cycling	Gabriel, Metatron
Dancing	Gabriel, Metatron, Raguel
Dining	Gabriel, Haniel, Raguel
DIY	Gabriel, Metatron, Uriel
Dog Breeding	Gabriel
Doll Making	Azriel, Chamuel, Gabriel, Jophiel, Uriel
Dolls' Houses and Miniatures	Azriel, Chamuel, Gabriel, Haniel, Jophiel, Uriel
Dominoes	Gabriel, Uriel
Drawing	Gabriel, Haniel, Metatron
Electronics	Gabriel, Michael
Embroidery	Azriel, Gabriel, Haniel, Jophiel, Uriel
Entertaining	Gabriel, Haniel, Raguel
Family	Gabriel, Haniel, Raguel, Raphael, Zadkiel
Fantasy Sports	Gabriel, Jophiel
Film-making	Azriel, Gabriel, Haniel, Jophiel, Uriel
Fine Wines	Gabriel
Fish Keeping	Ariel, Azriel, Gabriel, Raphael
Fishing	Ariel, Azriel, Gabriel
Fitness	Gabriel, Jeremiel, Metatron

Hobbies, Interests and Pastimes	Archangel
Food	Azriel, Gabriel
Football	Gabriel, Metatron, Raguel
Games	Gabriel, Metatron
Gardening	Gabriel, Haniel, Jophiel
Genealogy	Chamuel, Gabriel, Haniel, Sariel
Gliding	Gabriel, Metatron
Golf	Gabriel, Metatron
Grandchildren	Chamuel, Gabriel, Haniel, Metatron, Raphael, Zadkiel
Health	Gabriel, Haniel, Uriel, Zadkiel
Hi-Fi	Gabriel, Sandalphon
Hiking	Gabriel, Metatron
Historical Re-enactment	Gabriel, Metatron
History	Gabriel, Michael
Home Brewing	Gabriel, Haniel
Home Computing	Gabriel, Uriel
Homes	Gabriel, Haniel
Horse Riding	Ariel, Gabriel, Jophiel, Metatron, Raphael
Hunting	Gabriel, Raphael
Internet Surfing	Gabriel, Uriel
Jigsaw Puzzle	Chamuel, Haniel, Uriel
Kit-cars	Gabriel, Metatron, Uriel
Kite Flying	Gabriel, Jophiel, Metatron

HOBBIES, INTERESTS AND PASTIMES	ARCHANGEL
Knitting	Azriel, Gabriel, Uriel
Learning Foreign Languages	Gabriel, Michael
Lego	Chamuel, Gabriel, Haniel, Michael
Literature	Gabriel, Haniel, Metatron
Model Building	Azriel, Chamuel, Gabriel, Uriel
Modelling	Gabriel, Haniel
Motor Boats	Gabriel, Michael
Mountain Biking	Gabriel, Michael
Mountain Climbing	Gabriel, Michael
Musical Composition	Gabriel, Haniel, Jophiel, Metatron, Sandalphon, Uriel
Musician	Gabriel, Haniel, Metatron, Sandalphon, Uriel
Nature	Ariel, Gabriel, Jophiel, Metatron
Needlecraft	Azriel, Gabriel, Jophiel
Organic Gardening	Gabriel, Haniel, Michael
Outdoor activities	Gabriel, Metatron
Painting	Azriel, Gabriel, Haniel, Jophiel
Parenting	Gabriel, Jeremiel, Metatron, Raphael, Zadkiel
Patchwork	Azriel, Gabriel, Haniel, Uriel
Personal Development	Gabriel, Raphael, Raziel, Uriel, Zadkiel
Pets	Ariel, Gabriel, Jeremiel, Michael

Hobbies, Interests and Pastimes	Archangel
Photography	Azriel, Gabriel, Haniel, Jophiel
Playing Musical Instruments	Gabriel, Haniel, Raguel, Sandalphon
Postcards	Gabriel, Raguel
Puzzles	Chamuel, Gabriel, Haniel, Michael, Uriel
Quilting	Azriel, Gabriel, Haniel, Michael
Rafting	Ariel, Gabriel, Michael
Reading	Azriel, Gabriel, Sariel
Retail Therapy / Shopping	Metatron
Robotics	Gabriel, Metatron, Uriel
Role-playing Games	Gabriel, Raphael
Rugby	Gabriel, Metatron, Michael
Running	Gabriel, Metatron, Michael
Sailing	Ariel, Gabriel, Jophiel, Michael
Scrap Book Making	Gabriel, Haniel, Uriel
Sculpture	Azriel, Gabriel, Michael, Uriel
Sewing	Azriel, Gabriel, Uriel
Singing	Gabriel, Haniel, Metatron, Sandalphon, Uriel
Slimming	Gabriel, Metatron, Michael
Sports	Gabriel, Metatron, Michael
Stained Glass	Azriel, Gabriel, Uriel
Stamp Collecting	Gabriel, Michael, Raguel
Swimming	Ariel, Gabriel, Michael

Hobbies, Interests and Pastimes	Archangel
Team Games	Gabriel, Michael, Uriel
Television	Gabriel
Theatre	Gabriel, Sandalphon, Uriel
Toy Making	Azriel, Gabriel, Uriel
Trading Cards	Gabriel, Raguel
Train Spotting	Gabriel, Raguel
Travelling	Gabriel, Haniel, Jophiel, Michael
Trucks	Gabriel
Videos	Gabriel, Sandalphon
Walking	Gabriel, Jophiel, Michael
Wildlife	Ariel, Gabriel, Jophiel, Raphael
Woodcarving	Azriel, Gabriel, Haniel, Michael, Uriel
Woodworking	Azriel, Gabriel
Writing	Azriel, Gabriel, Jophiel, Metatron, Uriel
Yoga	Gabriel, Jeremiel, Michael, Raphael

ANGELS AND OCCUPATIONS

Can an archangel help you with your job? You bet! In fact many large corporations and companies have already recognized this fact. Archangel Michael, with his sword of protection, is the patron of soldiers and police officers as well as many other protection and support agencies!

Angels watch over all jobs and duties. Is your position listed here?

OCCUPATIONS	ARCHANGEL HELPER

A

Accountants and Auditors	Raguel, Metatron
Actors	Haniel, Gabriel, Zadkiel, Uriel
Administrative Law Judges, Adjudicators and Hearing Officers	Haniel, Gabriel, Raguel, Michael
Adult Literacy	Gabriel, Zadkiel, Uriel
Advertising Workers	Gabriel, Jophiel, Uriel
Aerospace Workers	Metatron, Michael
Agents and Business Managers of Artists, Performers and Athletes	Haniel, Gabriel, Zadkiel, Metatron, Uriel
Agricultural Workers	Ariel
Air Traffic Controllers	Chamuel, Haniel, Gabriel, Raphael, Uriel
Aircraft Workers	Haniel, Michael
Airline Pilots & Workers	Gabriel, Michael, Raphael, Uriel

Occupations	Archangel Helper
Ambulance Drivers and Attendants	Azrael, Zadkiel, Jeremiel, Michael, Raphael
Amusement and Recreation Attendants	Gabriel, Jophiel
Anaesthesiologists	Azrael, Haniel, Zadkiel, Michael, Raphael
Animal Breeders/Trainers	Haniel, Ariel, Uriel
Animal Control Workers	Chamuel, Ariel
Announcers	Haniel, Gabriel, Zadkiel, Uriel
Anthropologists and Archaeologists	Azrael, Ariel, Michael, Raphael
Arbitrators, Mediators and Conciliators	Haniel, Gabriel, Zadkiel, Michael
Architects & Architectural Workers	Ariel, Jophiel
Archivists, Curators and Museum Technicians	Azrael, Gabriel, Metatron, Uriel
Arts, Design, Drama, Entertainment, Music, Sports and Media Occupations	Haniel, Gabriel, Jophiel, Sandalphon, Uriel
Astrologers	Zadkiel, Jeremiel, Raphael, Raziel
Astronomers	Raphael, Raziel
Athletes	Haniel
Atmospheric, Earth, Marine and Space Sciences	Ariel, Raphael, Raziel, Uriel
Automotive & Body and Related Repairers	Haniel, Michael, Raphael

OCCUPATIONS	ARCHANGEL HELPER

B

Baggage Porters and Bellhops	Raguel, Raphael
Bailiffs	Jeremiel, Uriel
Bakers	Jophiel
Barbers	Chamuel
Bartenders	Gabriel, Ariel
Bicycle Repairers	Metatron, Michael
Biochemists and Biophysicists	Ariel, Raphael
Bookbinders	Michael
Bookkeeping, Accounting and Auditing Clerks	Gabriel, Raguel, Metatron, Uriel
Brickmasons and Blockmasons	Michael
Bridge and Lock Tenders	Ariel, Michael, Raphael
Broadcast Technicians	Gabriel, Michael
Brokerage Clerks	Raguel, Metatron
Budget Analysts	Gabriel
Building and Grounds Cleaning and Maintenance Occupations	Haniel, Michael
Bus Drivers	Raphael
Business and Financial Operations Occupations	Raguel
Butchers and Meat Cutters	Azrael

OCCUPATIONS	ARCHANGEL HELPER

Camera Operators	Gabriel
Captains, Mates and Pilots of Water Vessels	Ariel, Michael, Raphael
Cardiovascular Technologists and Technicians	Azrael, Raphael
Cargo and Freight Agents	Raguel
Carpenters	Haniel
Carpet Installers	Jophiel, Michael
Cartographers	Metatron
Cashiers	Zadkiel, Michael
Chefs and Head Cooks	Raguel, Jophiel
Chemical Workers	Haniel, Raphael
Chief Executives	Gabriel, Raguel
Child, Family and School Social Workers	Chamuel, Gabriel, Zadkiel, Michael, Sandalphon
Chiropractors	Jeremiel, Michael, Raphael
Choreographers	Haniel, Gabriel, Jophiel
Civil Engineering	Ariel, Jophiel
Claims Adjusters, Examiners and Investigators	Gabriel, Metatron
Cleaners & Washers-up	Raguel, Ariel, Michael

OCCUPATIONS	ARCHANGEL HELPER
Clergy	Azrael, Gabriel, Zadkiel, Metatron, Michael, Raziel
Clinical, Counselling and School Psychologists	Azrael, Chamuel, Gabriel, Zadkiel
Coaches	Haniel, Gabriel, Zadkiel
Coating, Painting, and Spraying Machine Setters and Operators	Jophiel, Michael
Coin, Vending and Amusement Machine Servicers and Repairers	Metatron, Michael
Combined Food Preparation and Serving Workers	Ariel
Commercial Divers	Ariel, Michael
Commercial and Industrial Designers	Uriel, Jophiel
Community and Social Services Occupations	Chamuel
Compensation, Benefits and Job Analysis Specialists	Gabriel, Jeremiel, Metatron
Compliance Officers	Raguel
Computer and Information Systems	Gabriel, Zadkiel, Metatron
Computer Controlled Machine Tool Operators, Metal and Plastic	Zadkiel
Concierges	Chamuel, Gabriel, Zadkiel
Conservation Scientists	Ariel, Raphael
Construction Workers	Michael
Construction and Building Inspectors	Chamuel, Gabriel

OCCUPATIONS	ARCHANGEL HELPER
Control and Valve Installers and Repairers	Michael
Cooks	Ariel
Cooling and Freezing Equipment Operators and Tenders	Ariel
Correctional Officers and Jailers	Chamuel, Zadkiel, Jeremiel, Michael
Correspondence Clerks	Gabriel, Metatron, Uriel
Cost Estimators	Zadkiel, Metatron
Counter Attendants, Cafeteria, Food Concession and Coffee Shop Operators	Zadkiel, Ariel
Couriers and Messengers	Gabriel, Zadkiel, Raphael
Court Reporters	Gabriel, Zadkiel, Metatron
Court, Municipal and License Clerks	Gabriel, Metatron
Crane and Tower Operators	Michael
Credit Analysts	Gabriel, Zadkiel, Metatron
Crossing Guards	Chamuel, Raguel, Michael
Customer Service Representatives	Gabriel, Zadkiel, Metatron
Cutters and Trimmers	Michael

Dancers	Haniel, Gabriel, Zadkiel, Sandalphon
Demonstrators and Product Promoters	Haniel, Gabriel, Zadkiel

OCCUPATIONS	ARCHANGEL HELPER
Dental Workers	Jeremiel
Derrick Operators, Oil and Gas	Michael
Desktop Publishers	Gabriel
Detectives and Criminal Investigators	Azrael, Gabriel, Zadkiel, Michael
Dieticians and Nutritionists	Haniel, Gabriel, Zadkiel, Metatron
Dining Room and Cafeteria Attendants and Bartender Helpers	Gabriel
Directors, Religious Activities and Education	Gabriel, Zadkiel, Michael
Dishwashers	Haniel, Ariel
Door-to-Door Sales Workers, News and Street Vendors and Related Workers	Gabriel, Michael
Dredger Operators	Ariel, Michael
Drilling and Boring Machine Tool Setters and Operators, Metal and Plastic	Michael
Driver/Sales Workers	Metatron, Raphael

Earth Drillers	Michael
Economists	Haniel, Gabriel, Zadkiel, Metatron
Editors	Haniel, Gabriel, Zadkiel, Metatron
Education Workers	Gabriel, Zadkiel, Metatron
Electrical Workers	Haniel, Michael

OCCUPATIONS	ARCHANGEL HELPER
Embalmers	Azrael
Emergency Medical Technicians and Paramedics	Azrael, Zadkiel, Jeremiel, Michael, Raphael, Sandalphon
Employment, Recruitment, and Placement Specialists	Haniel, Gabriel, Zadkiel, Metatron
Engine and Other Machine Assemblers	Metatron, Michael
Engineering Managers	Raguel
Environmental Engineering/Science	Haniel, Ariel, Raphael, Uriel
Etchers and Engravers	Haniel, Jophiel
Excavating and Loading Machine and Dragline Operators	Michael
Executive Secretaries and Administrative Assistants	Haniel, Gabriel, Zadkiel, Metatron
Explosives Workers, Ordnance Handling Experts and Blasters	Chamuel, Michael

Fabric Workers	Haniel, Jophiel
Family and General Practitioners	Azrael, Gabriel, Zadkiel, Raphael, Sandalphon
Farming, Fishing and Forestry Occupations	Ariel, Michael
Fashion Workers	Chamuel, Haniel, Gabriel, Jophiel
Fence Erectors	Chamuel, Michael

Occupations	Archangel Helper
Fibreglass Workers	Haniel
Film and Video Editors	Haniel, Gabriel, Jophiel
Financial Workers	Gabriel, Zadkiel, Metatron
Fine Artists, Including Painters, Sculptors and Illustrators	Haniel, Jophiel
Fire Fighters, Inspectors and Investigators	Azrael, Zadkiel, Ariel, Michael, Uriel
Fish and Game Wardens	Chamuel, Ariel, Michael
Fitness Trainers and Aerobics Instructors	Chamuel, Sandalphon
Flight Attendants	Gabriel, Raguel, Michael, Raphael
Floral Designers	Haniel, Gabriel, Jophiel
Food Preparation Workers	Ariel, Jophiel
Forensic Science Technicians	Azrael, Raphael
Forest Fire Inspectors and Prevention Specialists	Azrael, Chamuel, Ariel, Michael, Uriel
Foresters	Ariel, Michael
Funeral Directors	Azrael, Zadkiel, Jeremiel
Furniture Workers	Haniel

G

Gaming Workers	Zadkiel, Ariel
Gas Workers	Haniel, Michael

Occupations	Archangel Helper
General Managers	Gabriel, Zadkiel, Raguel, Metatron
Glaziers	Chamuel
Graphic Designers	Haniel, Gabriel, Jophiel

H

Hairdressers, Hairstylists and Beauticians	Chamuel, Jophiel
Hazardous Materials Removal Workers	Chamuel, Michael
Health Educators	Gabriel, Metatron, Uriel
Health and Safety Engineers (except Mining Safety Engineers and Inspectors)	Chamuel, Michael
Healthcare Workers	Azrael, Haniel, Zadkiel, Raphael
Heat Treating Equipment Setters and Operators, Metal and Plastic	Michael
Heating, Air Conditioning and Refrigeration Mechanics and Installers	Michael
Historians	Gabriel, Zadkiel, Metatron, Uriel
Hoist and Winch Operators	Michael
Home Appliance Repairers	Haniel, Metatron, Michael
Home Health Workers	Zadkiel, Jeremiel, Sandalphon
Hosts and Hostesses – Restaurants, Lounges, and Coffee Shops	Haniel, Gabriel, Raguel

OCCUPATIONS	ARCHANGEL HELPER
Hotel, Motel and Resort Desk Clerks	Haniel, Gabriel, Raguel
Human Resources Workers	Azrael, Gabriel, Zadkiel, Jeremiel, Metatron

I

Inspectors, Testers, Sorters, Samplers and Weighers	Haniel, Raguel, Metatron
Installation, Maintenance and Repair Occupations	Metatron, Michael
Insulation Workers	Michael
Insurance Workers	Zadkiel, Metatron
Interior Designers	Chamuel, Gabriel, Jophiel
Interpreters and Translators	Haniel, Gabriel, Zadkiel
Interviewers	Haniel, Gabriel, Zadkiel, Jeremiel, Metatron

J

Janitors and Cleaners	Haniel, Ariel
Jewellers and Precious Stone and Metal Workers	Haniel, Ariel, Jophiel
Judges and Magistrates	Azrael, Gabriel, Zadkiel, Metatron, Michael

Occupations	Archangel Helper

K L

Labourers	Jophiel
Landscaping and Groundskeeping Workers	Haniel, Ariel, Jophiel
Laundry and Dry Cleaning Workers	Raguel, Ariel
Legal Occupations	Azrael, Chamuel, Gabriel, Zadkiel, Metatron
Legislators	Haniel, Gabriel, Zadkiel, Metatron
Librarians	Gabriel, Zadkiel, Metatron, Uriel
Loading Machine Operators, Underground Mining	Ariel, Michael
Loan Officers	Gabriel, Metatron, Uriel
Locker Room, Coatroom and Dressing Room Attendants	Chamuel
Locksmiths and Safe Repairers	Chamuel, Metatron, Michael

M

Machinists	Michael
Maids and Housekeeping Cleaners	Haniel, Ariel
Maintenance Workers	Metatron, Michael
Make-up Artists, Theatrical and Performance	Chamuel, Haniel, Gabriel, Jophiel
Management	Haniel, Gabriel, Zadkiel, Metatron

OCCUPATIONS	ARCHANGEL HELPER
Manicurists and Pedicurists	Chamuel, Gabriel, Jophiel
Marine Engineers and Naval Architects	Ariel, Michael
Market Research Analysts	Gabriel, Zadkiel, Metatron,Uriel
Marketing	Haniel, Gabriel, Jophiel, Metatron,Uriel
Marriage and Family Therapists	Azrael, Haniel, Gabriel,Uriel
Massage Therapists	Jophiel
Meat, Poultry and Fish Cutters and Trimmers	Azrael
Mechanical Engineers	Metatron, Michael
Medical Workers	Azrael, Zadkiel, Sandalphon
Meeting and Convention Planners	Gabriel, Raguel, Metatron
Mental Health Workers	Azrael, Zadkiel, Jeremiel, Raphael
Merchandise Displayers and Window Trimmers	Haniel, Gabriel, Jophiel
Metal Workers	Michael
Meter Readers	Metatron
Microbiologists	Ariel, Raphael
Model Makers	Chamuel, Haniel, Jophiel
Models	Gabriel, Haniel, Jophiel
Motion Picture Projectionists	Haniel, Gabriel
Mould Makers	Haniel
Multi Media Artists and Animators	Haniel, Gabriel, Jophiel

OCCUPATIONS	ARCHANGEL HELPER
Musical Instrument Repairers and Tuners	Haniel, Gabriel, Metatron, Sandalphon
Musicians and Singers	Haniel, Gabriel, Jophiel, Sandalphon, Uriel

N

News Analysts, Reporters and Correspondents	Gabriel, Metatron, Uriel
Nuclear Technicians	Raguel, Ariel, Metatron, Michael, Raphael, Raziel
Nursing	Zadkiel, Jeremiel, Metatron, Raphael

O

Obstetricians and Gynaecologists	Gabriel, Zadkiel, Jeremiel, Raphael, Sandalphon
Occupational Health and Safety Specialists and Technicians	Chamuel, Metatron, Raphael, Uriel
Occupational Therapists	Zadkiel, Metatron, Raphael
Office Clerical	Haniel, Gabriel, Metatron
Operating Engineers and Other Construction Equipment Operators	Michael
Opticians	Zadkiel, Metatron, Raphael
Outdoor Power Equipment	Michael

OCCUPATIONS	ARCHANGEL HELPER

Packers and Packagers	Raguel
Painters	Haniel, Gabriel, Jophiel
Para-legals and Legal Assistants	Azrael, Gabriel, Zadkiel, Metatron
Parking/Traffic Warden	Chamuel, Metatron, Michael
Patternmakers	Haniel, Gabriel
Paving, Surfacing and Tamping Equipment Operators	Gabriel
Payroll and Timekeeping Clerks	Gabriel, Metatron
Paediatricians	Gabriel, Zadkiel, Raphael, Sandalphon
Personal Care and Service Occupations	Haniel
Personal Financial Advisors	Gabriel, Metatron
Personal and Home Care Aides	Zadkiel
Pest Control Workers	Chamuel
Pesticide Workers	Haniel
Petroleum Workers	Haniel, Michael
Pharmacists	Haniel, Metatron, Raphael
Pharmacy Technicians	Haniel, Metatron, Raphael, Uriel
Philosophy and Religious Teachers	Azrael, Gabriel, Zadkiel, Metatron, Michael
Photographic Workers	Haniel, Gabriel, Jophiel
Physical Therapists	Zadkiel, Jeremiel, Raphael

OCCUPATIONS	ARCHANGEL HELPER
Physician Assistants	Azrael, Zadkiel, Raphael, Uriel
Physicists	Raphael
Pile Driver Operators	Michael
Pipelayers	Michael
Plasterers and Stucco Masons	Haniel, Gabriel, Jophiel
Plumbers, Pipefitters and Steamfitters	Haniel, Ariel
Police	Chamuel, Zadkiel, Metatron, Michael, Uriel
Police, Fire and Ambulance Dispatchers	Azrael, Chamuel, Metatron, Michael, Uriel
Postal Workers	Gabriel, Metatron
Power Plant Workers	Michael
Printing Machine Operators	Michael
Private Detectives and Investigators	Chamuel, Gabriel, Metatron, Michael
Probation Officers and Correctional Treatment Specialists	Chamuel, Zadkiel, Michael
Producers and Directors	Haniel, Gabriel, Raguel
Production Workers	Raguel
Proofreaders and Copy Markers	Haniel, Gabriel, Metatron
Property and Community Association Managers	Raguel, Metatron
Protective Service Occupations	Michael
Psychiatric Workers	Chamuel, Zadkiel, Metatron, Raphael

OCCUPATIONS	ARCHANGEL HELPER
Public Relations Workers	Gabriel
Purchasing Workers	Gabriel, Metatron

Radiation Workers	Haniel, Michael, Raziel
Radio Workers	Haniel, Gabriel
Railway Workers	Michael
Receptionists and Information Clerks	Gabriel, Metatron, Uriel
Refuse and Recyclable Material Collectors	Michael
Retail Salespersons	Gabriel, Metatron
Roofers	Haniel

Sailors	Ariel, Michael
Sales	Gabriel, Metatron
Secretaries	Haniel, Gabriel, Metatron
Security and Fire Alarm Systems Workers	Chamuel, Michael
Service Station Attendants	Haniel, Michael
Set and Exhibit Designers	Haniel
Sewing Machine Operators	Haniel
Shampooers	Haniel, Ariel, Jophiel
Sheet Metal Workers	Michael

OCCUPATIONS	ARCHANGEL HELPER
Shipping Workers	Ariel, Michael
Shoe and Leather Workers and Repairers	Haniel
Skin-Care Specialists	Zadkiel, Jeremiel, Jophiel
Slaughterers and Meat Packers	Azrael
Social and Community Service Workers	Haniel, Gabriel, Raguel, Jeremiel, Metatron
Sound Engineering Technicians	Gabriel
Sports Competitors	Haniel
Stationary Engineers and Boiler Operators	Michael
Statisticians	Gabriel, Metatron
Stock Clerks and Order Fillers	Gabriel, Metatron
Stonemasons	Haniel, Jophiel
Structural Iron and Steel Workers	Jophiel, Michael
Substance Abuse and Behavioural Disorder Counsellors	Chamuel, Gabriel, Metatron, Michael
Surgical Workers	Zadkiel, Raphael,Uriel
Surveyors	Gabriel, Raguel, Metatron
Switchboard Operators	Gabriel, Zadkiel

Tailors, Dressmakers and Custom Sewers	Haniel, Gabriel, Jophiel
Taxidermists	Azrael
Taxi Drivers and Chauffeurs	Zadkiel, Raphael

OCCUPATIONS	ARCHANGEL HELPER
Teachers	Gabriel, Zadkiel, Uriel
Telecommunications Workers	Gabriel, Metatron
Telemarketers	Gabriel, Metatron
Telephone Operators	Gabriel
Textile Workers	Haniel, Gabriel
Tour Guides and Escorts	Gabriel, Zadkiel, Metatron, Raphael
Traffic Technicians	Chamuel, Michael, Raphael
Training and Development Workers	Gabriel, Jeremiel, Metatron
Travel Workers	Gabriel, Metatron, Raphael
Tree Surgeons	Ariel, Michael
Truck/Van Drivers	Raphael
Tyre Repairers and Changers	Michael

U

Umpires, Referees and Other Sports Officials	Chamuel, Haniel, Gabriel, Metatron
Undertakers	Azrael, Jeremiel, Michael, Sandalphon
Upholsterers	Haniel, Jophiel
Urban and Regional Planners	Zadkiel, Raguel, Ariel, Metatron
Ushers, Lobby Attendants and Ticket Takers	Chamuel, Gabriel

OCCUPATIONS	ARCHANGEL HELPER

V

Veterinary Workers	Azrael, Ariel

W

Waiters and Waitresses	Gabriel
Watch Repairers	Metatron, Michael
Water and Liquid Waste Treatment Workers	Ariel, Michael
Weighers, Measurers, Checkers and Samplers, Recordkeeping	Metatron
Welding, Soldering and Brazing Machine Setters and Operators	Michael
Wholesale and Retail Buyers	Gabriel, Metatron
Woodworking Workers	Jophiel
Writers and Authors	Gabriel, Jophiel, Metatron, Uriel

X Y Z

Zoologists and Wildlife Biologists	Ariel, Michael, Raphael

ARCHANGELS AND THEIR PLANETS

Each archangel has charge over the different planets. As with the other designated roles, different religions and traditions have different interpretations! (*See* 'angels and astrology' for the 'angels of the hours' and how they relate to the planets)

PLANET	ARCHANGEL
Sun	Raphael/Michael
Moon	Gabriel
Mercury	Michael/Raphael
Venus	Haniel/Aniel
Mars	Kamael/Samael
Jupiter	Tzadkiel/Zadkiel/Sachiel
Saturn	Zadkiel/Kafziel/Cassiel
Uranus	Ariel (the name of one of Uranus' 'satellites!')
Pluto	Michael
Neptune	Ariel/Azrael
Sedna*	Ariel/Azrael

* Sedna is the recently discovered 'ice planet', named after the Inuit goddess of the ocean.

ANGELS OF PUNISHMENT

Yes, there are angels of punishment according to *The Testament of Solomon*. These are under the guidance and direction of the archangels. These angels are given charge over 'the seven divisions of hell'.

ANGEL NAME	MEANING OF NAME
Kushiel	Rigid one of God
Lahatiel	Flaming one of God
Shoftiel	Judge of God
Makatiel	Plague of God
Hutriel	Rod of God
Pusiel/Puriel	Fire of God
Rogziel	Wrath of God

ANGELS OF THE SEASONS

Do you need an archangel to help with a specific time of year? Choose one of the following, as appropriate.

SEASON	ARCHANGEL
Spring	Raphael
Summer	Ariel
Autumn	Michael
Winter	Gabriel

ANGELS OF THE WEEK

Angels can also help with different days of the week. As with other angelic information, different sources list different angels to rule over each day.

DAY OF THE WEEK	ARCHANGEL	ANGEL
Monday	Gabriel	Gabriel
Tuesday	Camael	Zamael
Wednesday	Michael	Raphael
Thursday	Tzadkiel	Sachiel
Friday	Haniel	Anael
Saturday	Tzaphiel	Cassiel
Sunday	Raphael	Michael

ANGELS OF THE WINDS

There are generally said to be four angels in charge of the direction of the winds – one archangel for each direction. In the *Third Book of Enoch*, the angel Za'afiel is named as the angel who is in charge of 'whirlwinds'. Za'afiel is the angel of hurricanes … just in case you need them!

DIRECTION OF WINDS	ARCHANGEL IN CHARGE
North	Michael
South	Raphael
East (and North)	Ariel/Uriel
West	Gabriel

ANGELS OF THE ZODIAC

Which angel looks over your birth sign?

BIRTH SIGN	ANGEL IN CHARGE
Capricorn	Hanael
Aquarius	Cambiel
Pisces	Barchiel
Aries	Machidiel
Taurus	Asmodel
Gemini	Ambriel
Cancer	Muriel
Leo	Verchiel
Virgo	Hamaliel
Libra	Uriel
Scorpio	Barbiel
Sagittarius	Adnachiel

3

Angel Names A–Z

Angel Names A–Z

A
ngel names come from hundreds of sources, including religious texts, traditional tales or folklore, and magical and mystical references. One of the most important of these sources is the Jewish mystical tradition known as Kabbalah (or Qabalah, according to some; Cabbalah according to others! However it is spelled, the word means 'received', as in 'received wisdom' handed down over the ages). Some angels have many different names according to which part of the world you are from or which source you reference. Spellings vary so much that it is hard to know if you are dealing with several angels or the same angel with different names! Where I could find variations, I have listed them here.

Some of the angels with the more obscure or occult references have not been included in this list, but I have decided to add the fallen angels – even though many sources leave them out altogether.

Is this the 'ultimate' list of angel names? I doubt it, but it's probably a big enough list for normal reference!

A'albiel	An angel who works for Archangel Michael
Abachta	One of the seven angels of confusion mentioned in rabbinic writings
Abaddon	The 'angel of the bottomless pit' or 'Destroyer,' mentioned in *Revelation* 9. Also known as 'death's dark angel' in Handel's oratorio *The Messiah*
Aban	Angel of October, according to Persian legend.
Abariel	An invoking angel
Abasdarhon	Angel of the 5th hour of the night
Abay	An angel from the hierarchical order of dominions
Abbadoba	A seraph and a fallen angel
Abdia	An angel appearing on the pentagram of Solomon.
Abdiel	Meaning 'Servant of God'. Abdiel is mentioned in *The Book of the Angel Raziel*, (written in the middle ages). Abdiel is also known as the 'flaming seraph'
Abdizriel	Mentioned in the Kabbalah as one of 28 angels ruling the mansions of the moon
Abedumabal	An angel called upon in magical prayer
Abel	One of the angels of the 4th heaven, and an angel of the order of Powers in the angelic Hierarchy

Abelech	An angel who is called to manage demons
Abezi-Thirbod	Also known as Samael
Abheiel	Abheiel is one of the angels ruling the 28 mansions of the moon
Aboezra	An angel named in the *Book of Ceremonial Magic*
Abrasiel	An angel of the 7th hour of the day
Abrid	An angel of the Summer Equinox
Abriel	One of the angels of the Dominions
Abrimas	An angel called to close the Sabbath
Abru-El	Also known as Gabriel
Abrunael	One of the angels ruling the 28 Mansions of the moon
Abuionij	An angel of the 2nd heaven
Abuiori	Abuiori is one of the angels over Wednesday
Abuliel	An angel who controls the relaying of prayer in Jewish tradition
Abuzohar	An angel of the moon – looking after Monday
Achaiah	One of the 8 seraphim mentioned in the Kabbalah
Acrabiel	Acrabiel rules over one of the signs of the zodiac
Adabiel	According to some sources, one of the 7 archangels
Adadiyah	Also known as Metatron
Adeo	One of the angels of the order of the dominions

Adhar	Also known as Metatron
Adiriel	An angel of the 5th heaven
Admael	According to some sources one of the 7 archangels who takes care of the earth
Adnachiel	An angel of November
Adnarel	Adnarel means, 'My Lord is God', an overseer of Winter
Adonael	Sometimes named as one of the 7 archangels
Adoniel	Named as an angel over the 12th hour of night
Adoyahel	A ministering throne angel mentioned in the Kabbalah
Adrael	Name means 'My help is God'. An angel of the 1st heaven
Adrapen	An angel of the 9th hour of night
Adriel	One of the angels ruling the 28 mansions of the moon
Adrigon	Also known as Metatron
Aebel	One of three angels who looked after Adam.
Af	Whose name means 'anger' and named as an angel of destruction
Afafiel	A guard of the hall of the 7th heaven
Afkiel	A guard of the hall of the 5th heaven
Aftiel	The angel of twilight
Agad	An angel from the hierarchical order of the Powers

Agares	From the order of Virtues
Agbas	A guard of the hall of the 4th heaven
Agkagdiel	A guard of the hall of the 7th heaven
Agrat bat Mahlat	Angel of prostitution
Agromiel	A guard of the 6th heaven
Aha	An angel from the order of the Dominions
Ahariel	A ruler of the 2nd day
Aiavel	One of the angels over the zodiac
Aiel	Aiel is an angel of the air and one of the zodiac angels
Aker	A judging angel to be present at the end of the world
Akriel	An angel overseeing the infertile
Alfatha	An angel of the North
Almon	A guard of the 4th heaven
Alphiel	An angel who oversees fruit trees
Altarib	An angel of winter
Amaliel	An angel of punishment
Amatiel	An angel over spring
Ambriel	One of the angels of the month of May

Appolion	Also known as Abbadon
Ariel	Whose name means 'Lion of God' and one of the 7 archangels
Auriel	Another name for Oriel ('Light of God')
Azazel	Chieftain of the fallen angels according to the *Book of Enoch*

Belair	Meaning 'Worthless,' the angel of lawlessness
Beliel	A fallen angel
Belphegor	An angel of the order of Principalities
Belsal	Belsal is an angel of the 1st hour of the night
Belzeboub	Prince of the Seraphim (although not strictly an angel but a demon)
Bencul	A Kabbalistic angel
Beniel	An angel who bestows the gift of invisibility
Beratiel	An angel of the 12th hour of the day
Bernael	Angel of darkness
Bethuael	Whose name means 'House of God'
Bezriel	A guardian of the 3rd heaven
Bibiyah	Another name for archangel Metatron

Bifiel	One of the guardians of the 6th heavenly hall
Bigtha	An angel of confusion (one of 7)
Blaef	An angel ruling over Fridays
Bne Seraphim	One of the angels of the planet Mercury and in some references also Venus
Bodiel	Prince of the 6th heaven
Boel	Whose name means 'God is in him'; one of 7 throne angels who resides in the 7th heaven
Buhair	An angel whose role is to follow the path of the sun (one of 10)
Burchat	An angel of the air who resides in the 4th heaven
Busasjal	One of the fallen angels

Cabiel	One of the 28 angels ruling over the mansions of the moon
Cabriel	An angel of Aquarius
Cahethel	A member of the seraphim who watches over crops
Calliel	An angel of the throne who resides in the 2nd heaven
Caluel	An angel over Wednesday who resides in either the 2nd or the 3rd heaven
Calzas	One of the Tuesday angels

Camael	Often regarded as the chief of the order of Powers. In Kabbalistic law is considered one of the ten archangels. One of various spellings of the name which means 'He Who Sees God'
Camal	'To Desire God'; an archangel of the Kabbalah
Cambiel	An angel of the 9th hour, presides over the zodiac sign of Aquarius
Cambill	Angel of the 8th hour of the night
Capabile	A sun messenger
Capabili	Angel of the 4th heaven
Caracasa	An angel of Spring
Carcas	One of the seven angels of confusion
Cassiel	An angel of the order of Powers also known as the angel of temperance, and an angel of Saturdays
Castiel	A Thursday angel
Casujoiah	An angel of the zodiac sign of Capricorn
Cernaiul	An angel of the 7th sefiroth
Cetarari	An angel who presides over Winter
Chabril	Watches over the 2nd hour of night
Chamuel	'He who seeks God'; one of the archangels
Charby	An angel of the 5th hour
Charciel	An angel of the 4th heaven

Charman	One of the angels of the 11th hour of the night
Charmeas	An angel of the 1st hour of the day
Charms	One of the angels of the 9th hour of the day
Charnij	An angel of the 10th hour of the day
Charpon	An angel of the 1st hour of the day
Charuch	One of the angels of the 6th hour of the day
Chasdiel	One of many names for the angel Metatron
Chastiser	A destroying angel
Chedustaniel	An angel over Fridays
Cheratiel	An angel of the 6th hour of night
Chermes	One of the angels of the 9th hour of night
Chermiel	An angel over Fridays
Chesetial	One of the angels of the zodiac
Choriel	Angel of the 8th hour of the day
Chorob	Angel of the 10th hour of the day
Chrymos	An angel ruling over the 5th hour of night
Chuabotheij	An angel of the seal
Chuscha	One of the Throne angels
Chushiel	One of the angels who guard the gate of the South Wind

Cogediel	An angel of the 28 mansions of the moon
Comadiel	One of the 3rd hour of the day angels
Comary	An angel over the 9th hour of the night
Commissoros	One of the angels over Spring
Corabael	An angel who rules over Mondays
Corat	This angel resides in the 3rd heaven who looks after Fridays
Core	An angel who looks after the season of Spring
Coriel	One of the angels of the 7th hour of night
Cosel	An angel who watches over the 1st hour of night
Crociel	One of the angels over the 7th hours of the day
Cruciel	An angel of the 3rd Hour of the night
Ctarari	One of two angels who look over the season of Winter
Curaniel	Looks after Mondays

Dabriel	Dabriel looks after Mondays and resides in the 1st heaven. Known as a heavenly scribe
Daden	This angel resides in the 6th heaven
Dagiel	An angel who looks after fish

Dagymiel	One of the angels who look after the zodiac
Dahavauron	An angel who resides in the 3rd heaven and is also an angel-guard
Dahaviel	A guard of the 1st Heaven
Dalkiel	An angel of Hell
Damabiath	This is one of the angels of the order of Powers
Dameal	An angel of Tuesdays
Damiel	One of the angels of the 5th hour
Daniel	Whose name means 'God is my Judge'; one of the angels of the order of the Principalities
Dara	An angel who looks over rivers and rains
Darbiel	One of the angels of the 10th hours of the day
Dardariel	A ruling angel of the 11th hour of the night
Daresiel	An angel of the 1st hour of the day
Darkiel	An angel guard over the South Wind gates
Darmosiel	One of the angels over the 12th hour of night
Darquiel	This is one of the angels who looks after Mondays
Deharhiel	One of the guards of the 5th heavenly hall
Delukiel	An angelic guard of the 7th heaven
Deramiel	One of the angels over the 3rd heaven

Didnaor	One of the angels listed in *The Book of Angel Raziel*
Dina	Dina is a guardian angel who presides over law and wisdom
Dirachiel	An angel over the 28 mansions of the moon
Dirael	One of the guards of the 6th heavenly hall
Djibril	Also known as Gabriel, the archangel messenger
Domiel	One of the angels who guard the 6th hall of the 7th heaven
Donel	A guard of the guards of the gates of the South Wind
Doremiel	An angel of the North that looks after Fridays
Dormiel	An angel guard who looks after the gates of the East Wind
Dracon	One of the angels of the 6th hour of the night
Dramazod	An angel of the 6th hour of the night
Dramozin	One of the angels of the 8th hour of the night
Drelmeth	An angel of the 3rd hour of the day
Drial	An angel guard of the 5th heaven
Drsmiel	Known as an evil angel
Dubbiel	One of the guardian angels of Persia
Duma	The angel of silence
Dumariel	An angel of the 11th hour of the night
Durba'il	Invoked in rites of exorcism, a guardian angel in Arabic Law

Ebed	Another name for Metatron
Eblis	Whose name means 'Despair'; an evil angel
Efniel	From the order of the Cherabim
Egibiel	One of the angels over the 28 mansions of the moon
Egion	A guardian of the 7th heavenly hall
Egrimiel	A guardian of the 6th heavenly hall
El El	A guard over the gates of the North Wind
Eladel	One of the angels of the zodiac
Elamiz	An angel of the 11th hour of the night
Elemiah	One of the seraphim of the tree of life
Elimelech	Whose name means 'My God Is King'; an angel of summer
Elimiel	The angel of the moon
Elion	Resides in the 1st heaven
Eloeus	An angel of the presence
Elogium	Rules over the month of September
Eloha	One of the order of Powers
Eloheij	An angel of the Seal

Elubatel	An angel of omnipotence
Emmanuel	Whose name means 'God With Us'; the angel in the fiery furnace
Enediel	One of the angels of the 28 mansions of the moon
Erastiel	An angel of the 5th heaven
Eremiel	This angel looks after souls in the underworld
Ergedial	One of the angels governing the 28 mansions of the moon
Ermosiel	An angel of the 2nd hour
Ertrael	A fallen angel
Esabiel	An angel of the order of Powers
Eschiros	An angel of the 7 planets
Estes	Also known as Metatron
Eth	This angel acts as a Time Lord
Etraphill	A trumpeter to be called on the Last Day of Judgement
Etremphsuchos	A angel guardian over the 7 heavens
Eurabatras	Presides over the planet Venus
Eved	Also known as Metatron
Exael	This angel taught humans how to create works in silver and gold and gems and perfumes

Ezeqeel	Whose name means 'Strength of God'; a fallen angel
Ezrael	Whose name means 'Help of God' and 'Angel of Wrath'

Fabriel	An angel of the 4th heaven
Fakr-Ed-Din	'Poor One of Faith'. In the Yezidic religion an archangel
Famiel	An angel of the Air, who resides in the 3rd heaven, a Friday angel
Fanuel	One of the angels of the Presence
Farrias	An angel of the 2nd hour of the night
Farun Faro Vakshur	A guardian angel
Farvardin	An angel of March who watches over the 19th day of each month, a member of the Cherabim
Focalor	An angel of the order of thrones
Forcas	A fallen angel
Forneus	One of the fallen angels
Fraciel	A Tuesday angel of the 5th heaven
Framoch	This angel watches over the 7th hour of the night
Fremiel	An angel of the 4th hour of the night
Friagne	A Tuesday angel residing on the 5th heaven

Fromezin	An angel of the 2nd hour of the night
Fromzon	An angel of the 3rd hour of the night
Fuleriel	Watching over the 6th hour of the night
Furiel	An angel of the 3rd hour of the day
Furlac	An earth angel
Furmiel	Serving under Bariel, an angel of the 11th hour of the day
Fustriel	Over the 5th hour of the day
Futiniel	An angel of the 5th hour of the day

G

Gaap	A fallen angel
Gabriel	One of four archangels named in Hebrew tradition. Thought to be one of the highest ranking angels and the messenger that brought the word of her pregnancy to Mary, mother of Jesus. Name means 'God is My Strength'
Gabuthelon	An angel who will supervise at the end of the world
Gader	An angel guard of the 4th heavenly hall
Gadhiel	An angel guarding the 6th heaven
Gadreel	Whose name means 'God is My Helper'; a fallen angel
Gadriel	The chief ruling angel of the 5th heaven, also in charge of wars among nations

Ga'ga	An angel guard of the 7th heavenly hall
Galdel	An angel of the 5th heaven. A Tuesday angel
Galgaliel	An angel of the Sun
Galiel	Also know as Metatron
Galizur	An angel Moses encountered in heaven, ruling prince of the 2nd heaven
Galmon	An angel guard of the 4th heavenly hall
Gambiel	Ruler of the Astrological sign Aquarius
Gambriel	An angel of the 5th heaven
Gamiel	An angel of the 1st hour of the night
Gamrial	A warden of the 7 celestial halls
Gamsiel	An angel of the 8th hour of the night
Ganael	One of the 7 planetary rulers
Garfial	Guardian of the 5th heaven
Gargatel	Presides over Summer
Gariel	A guard of the 5th heaven
Garthiel	Ruler of the 1st hour of the night
Gastrion	An angel of the 8th hour of the night
Gatiel	A guard of the 5th heaven
Gaviel	Serves as one of the 3 angels of the Summer

Gavreel	Angelic guard of the East Wind
Gazardiel	A Talmudic angel in charge of the rising and setting of the Sun
Gazarniel	An angel of the 'Flame of Fire'
Geal	A guard of the 5th heaven
Gedael	Name means 'Fortune of God', governing angel of the Zodiac
Gedariah	An angel of the 3rd heaven
Gedudiel	A guard of the 7th heaven
Gehatsitsa	Stationed at the 5th heaven
Gehegiel	Resides over the 6th heaven
Gehirael	A guardian of the 7th heavenly hall
Geliel	One of the governing angels of the 28 mansions of the Moon
Geminiel	A governing angel of the Zodiac
Genaritzod	Chief angel over the 7th hour of the night
Geno	An angel of the order of Powers
Gergot	An angelic guard of the 6th heavenly hall
Germael	Whose name means 'Majesty of God'; sent by God to create Adam from the dust
Geroskesufael	A guard of the 7th heaven
Gethel	Looks for hidden things

Gezuriya	A guard of the 7 Celestial Halls
Glaras	Watches over the 1st hour of the night
Gloarig	An angel of the 3rd hour of the day
Gmial	A warden of the 7 Celestial Halls
Goap	A fallen angel
Gonael	A guard of the North Wind
Gorfiniel	A guard of the 7th heaven
Graniel	An angel of the 2nd hour
Granozin	An angel of the 2nd hour of the night
Grial	A guardian of the 5th heaven
Gualbarel	An angel of Autumn
Guael	Angel of the 5th heaven, who rules on Tuesdays
Gurid	An angel of the Summer Equinox
Guriel	Whose name means 'Welp of God'; an angel ruling the astrological sign of Leo
Guth	An angel of the planet Jupiter
Gutrix	An angel of the air and of Thursdays
Guziel	An evil angel
Gvurtial	A guard of the 4th heaven

H

Haael   One of the angels of the Zodiac

Haaiah   An angel of the Dominion order

Haamiah   Angel of the order of Powers

Habbiel   Angel of the 1st heaven, ruling over Mondays

Habriel   Angel of the order of Powers

Hachashel   One of the angels of the Zodiac

Hadakiel   Rules over the sign of Libra

Hadasdagedoy   A guard of the 6th Heaven

Hadraniel   'Majesty' or 'Greatness of God'; a guard of the 2nd heaven

Haduriel   A ruling guard of the 6th heavenly hall

Hagai   An angel guard of the 5th heaven

Hagedola   An angel of the Seal

Haggo   An angel of the Seal

Haglon   An angel of the 3rd hour of the night

Hahael   Hahael is an angel of the order of the Virtues

Hahaiah   From order of Cherubim, Hahaiha reveals hidden mysteries and influences thoughts of humans

Hahayel	A ministering angel who sits on the Divine Judgment Council
Hahiniah	A throne angel
Hahowel	A ministering angel
Haiaiel	One of the 72 angels of the Zodiac
Hailiel	An angel chief of the order of Hayyoth (holy beasts)
Haim	Presides over the Zodiac sign Virgo
Hakamiah	Invoked against traitors, a guardian angel of France and a member of the Cherubim
Hakem	An angel guard of the 4th heaven
Hakha	One of many angels of the Seal
Hakham	Also known as Metatron
Halacho	A Genii of the 11th hour
Halelviel	An angel guard of the 7th heaven
Halqim	A guard of the gates of the North Wind
Haludiel	An intelligence of the Sun, an angel of the 4th heaven
Halwaya	A secret name for Metatron
Hamabiel	Rules of the zodiac sign of Taurus
Hamal	This angel watches over water
Hamaliel	An angel of the order of Virtues who rules over the sign of Virgo and the month of August

Hamarytzod	Angel of the 11th hour
Hamatiel	Rules over the sign of Virgo
Hamaya	One of many ministering angels
Hamayzod	An angel of the 4th hour of the night
Hameriel	An angel of the 5th hour of the night
Ham Meyuchad	A member of the order of the Cherubim
Hamneijs	One of many angels of the Seal
Hamon	Also known as Gabriel. An angelic guard of the gates of the South Wind
Hanaeb	Listed as one of the angels of the Zodiac
Hanalel	A fallen angel
Hananiel	Name means 'Graciously Given of God'. Some traditions recognize him as an archangel
Hanhl	Balaam ordered Hanhl to build the first 7 altars
Haniel	Whose name means 'Glory' or 'Grace of God'; also known as Aniel. Angel of the month of December
Hannuel	Rules over the sign of Capricorn
Hanoziz	Rules over the 8th hour of the night
Hanozoz	An angel of the 9th hour of the night
Hantiel	Watches over the 3rd hour of the day

Hanum	Rules over Mondays, resides in the 1st heaven
Haqemel	One of the angels of the Zodiac
Harabael	An angel guardian of the earth
Harahel	Watches over the heavenly archives
Harbonah	One of the angels of confusion, whose name means 'Ass Driver'
Harhaziel	A protector of the 3rd heaven
Harial	Watches over domestic animals, a member of the Cherubim, watches over science and arts
Hariph	Also known as Raphael
Haris	Also known as Iblis, leader of the fallen angels in Arabic tradition
Hariton	A fictional archangel
Harta'il	A guardian angel called upon in rites of exorcism in Arabic Lore
Harudha	A mythological angel who rules over water
Harut	A fallen angel associated with Murut
Harviel	An angelic guard of the 2nd heaven
Hasdiel	Angel over the planet Venus, also an angel of benevolence
Haseha	A throne angel
Hashesiyah	Also known as Metatron
Hasmed	The angel of annihilation

Hasmiyah	Also known as Metatron
Hatspatsiel	Also known as Metatron
Haurvatat	Name means 'Wholeness'; a Persian archangel
Haven	The genius of Dignity who watches over the 12 hours of the day
Haziel	Name means 'Vision of God'; a member of the Cherubim
He'il	Name means 'Life of God'
Heiglot	An angel of snow storms, a ruler of the 1st hour
Helel	A fallen angel
Helison	An angel of the 1st Altitude
Hemah	An angel of Wrath; watches over the passing of domestic animals, also recognized as an angel of destruction
Hermesiel	A ruler over the heavenly choir
Heziel	One of the angels of the Zodiac
Hilin Hntr	An angel of the Winds
Hilofatei	A guard of the 4th heaven
Hipeton	Watches over the planet Jupiter
Hizkiel	An aide to archangel Gabriel
Hlk Lil **Hlk Lib**	An angel of Holiness
Hngel	One of the Summer Equinox angels

Hochmel	Whose name means 'Wisdom of God'; the inspirer of the *Grimoire of Pope Honorius III*
Hodiel	'Victory of God'; an angel of the world of creation
Hodiriron	One of the 10 holy sefiroth
Hodniel	An angel of curing 'stupidity' in humans
Hofniel	Translates to 'Fighter for God'; chief of the Sons of God
Homadiel	'The Angel of the Lord'
Hormuz	Rules over the 1st day of the month
Hosampsich	A leader of the fallen angels
Hubaiel	An angel of the 1st heaven
Hubaril	An angelic guard of the planet Saturn
Hufaltiel	An angel of the 3rd heaven who watches over Fridays
Hukiel	An guardian of the 7th heaven
Hula'il	Called for rites of exorcism in Arabic lore
Humastrav	An angel who watches over Mondays
Humiel	This angel is one who watches over the sign of Capricorn
Huphatriel	One of the angels of the planet Jupiter
Hurtapal	An angel of the Lord's Day
Husael	Watches over the 3rd heaven

Hutriel	Whose name means 'Rod of God'; an angel of punishment
Huzia	An angel of the 7 Celestial Halls
Hyniel	A Tuesday angel

I

Iadara	Watches over the zodiac sign of Virgo
Iahmel	This angel is one of the angels of the Air
Ialcoajul	An angel of the 11th hour of the night
Iamariel	Angel of the 9th hour of the night
Iaoth	One of the 7 archangels according to *The Testament of Solomon*
Iaqwiel	An angel of the moon
Iciriel	One of the angels ruling the 28 mansions of the moon
Idrael	A guard of the 5th heaven
Iehuiah	Belonging to the order of the Thrones
Ieiaiel	Watches over the future
Ielahiah	Works with the law and protects legal workers
Ierimiel	Also known as Jeremiel
Iesaea	Also known as Metatron
Ilaniel	A guardian of fruit-bearing trees

Iofiel	Whose name means 'Beauty of God'; recognized by some as one of the 7 archangels.
Ishliah	An angel of the East
Israel	Whose name means 'Striver with God'; a Throne angel
Israfil	Also known as Israfel, whose name means 'The Burning One'; one of the four archangels of Islam, the angel of resurrection
Itqal	An angel of affection
Iurabatres	A guardian of the planet Venus
Iz'iel	A guard of the 6th heaven
Izrael	Along with Gabriel, Michael and Israfel, will be exempt from the blast of the 1st trumpet of Judgment Day
Izra'il	The Muslim angel of death and one of the four archangels of Islam

Jabniel	An angel of the 3rd heaven
Jachniel	An angel guard of the South Wind
Janax	A guardian of Mondays
Janiel	A guardian of Tuesdays and an angel of the 5th heaven
Jariel	An angel of the Presence
Javan	A guardian angel of Greece

Jazeriel	One of the angels of the 28 mansions of the moon
Jehoel	One of the Princes of the Presence and chief of the order of the seraphim
Jehudiel	A Governor of the Celestial Spheres
Jekusiel	An angel guard of the 1st heaven
Jerazol	An angel of Power
Jeremiel	Whose name means 'Mercy of God'; sometimes listed as one of the 7 archangels
Jerescue	A governing angel of Wednesdays
Jesodoth	Channels wisdom directly from the source to humankind.
Jetrel	One of the fallen angels
Jeu	This angel governs over the Cosmos
Jibril	Also known as Gabriel
Joel	An archangel credited with requesting that Adam name all things, *Genesis* 2:19-20
Johiel	Angel of Paradise
Jomjael	A fallen angel
Joustriel	An angel of the 6th hour of the day
Jove	A fallen angel
Jusjuarin	An angel of the 10th hour of the night

Kadashiel	A guard of the gates of the South Wind
Kadiel	An angel from the 3rd heaven who rules over Fridays
Kadkadael	A guard of the 6th heavenly hall
Kadosh	A guard of the 4th heavenly hall
Kafziel	Whose name means 'Speed of God'; in some traditions is named as an archangel
Kakabel	An angel in charge of the stars and constellations
Karmiel	An angel of the gates of the East Wind
Kartion	A guard of the 7th heaven
Kasdaye	A fallen angel
Kaseel	A angel of sin
Kashiel	One of the angels of the gates of the South Wind
Kashriel	A guard of the 1st heaven
Katzfiel	Prince of the Sword, guard of the 6th heaven
Katzmiel	Guard angel, stationed in the 6th heaven
Kavzakiel	An angel prince of the Sword
Kazviel	Guardian angel of the 4th heaven

Keel	Name means 'Like God'; one of the angels of the Seasons
Kemuel	Also known as Chamuel, name means 'Assembly of God'; a gatekeeper of heaven
Kerubiel	Head of the Order of the Cherubim
Ketheriel	Name means 'Crown of God'
Keveqel	An angel of the zodiac
Kezef	An angel of Death
Kfial	A warden angel of the 7 Celestial Halls
Khurdad	In ancient Persia the angel of May
Kinor	An angel positioned at the ancient gates of hell
Kiramu 'l-katibin	A recording angel
Kirtabus	A genii of the 9th hour
Kisael	A guardian of the 5th heavenly hall
Klaha	A guardian of the gates of the South Wind
Kmiel	An angel of the Summer Equinox
Kolazonta	A destroying angel
Korniel	An angel guard of the South Wind
Kso'ppghiel	An angel of fury
Kushiel	Name means 'Rigid One of God'; an angel of punishment

Kutiel	This angel is called when using the divining rods
Kyniel	An angel of the 3rd heaven
Kyriel	One of the angels of the 28 mansions of the moon
Kzuial	An guardian of the 4th heaven

Labarfiel	A guard of the 7th heaven
Labbiel	Also known as Raphael
Labusi	An angel of omnipotence
Lahash	An angel who tried to stop a prayer sent my Moses from reaching God
Lahatiel	'The flaming one'; an angel of punishment
Lailah	In Jewish legend is the angel of night and looks after conception
Lama	Ruler of Tuesdays, an angel of the air
Lamach	Watchers over the planet Mars
Lamediel	An angel of the 4th hour of the night
Lecabel	Watches over agriculture
Ledrion	This angel can be called during exorcism
Lehavah	Angelic guard of the 7th heaven

Lelahel	Watches over love, art, science and fortune
Leliel	An angel ruler of the night
Librabis	A genii of the 7th hour
Lifton	An angel guard of the 7th heaven
Little Iao	Also known as Metatron
Liwet	Angel of love and invention according to Mandaean Law
Lobkir	An angel guard of the gates of the West Wind
Lobquin	An angel of the 5th heaven who rules on Tuesdays in the West
Loel	A guard of the gates of the South Wind
Loquel	Resides in the 1st heaven
Lucifer	Whose name means 'Light Giver' and is often equated (some say mistakenly) with the fallen angel Satan

Machasiel	An angel residing in the 4th heaven who rules on the 4th day, also known as an Intelligence of the Sun
Machathan	Has guardianship of the Air, rules over Saturdays
Machidiel	Whose name means 'Fullness of God'; an angel of the month of March and the star sign Aries
Machnia	A guard of the gates of the South Wind

Madan	Ruler of the planet Mercury
Mador	A guard of the 4th heaven
Madriel	Watches over the 9th hour of the day
Mael	Rules over the planet Saturn, also a Monday angel
Maguth	Presides over Thursdays and is an angel of the Air
Mahananel	A guard of the gates of the North Wind
Mahariel	Whose name means 'Swift'; an angel of paradise
Maianiel	Angel serving in the 5th heaven, listed in the 6th and 7th book of Moses
Maion	A ruler of the planet Saturn
Makatiel	Whose name means 'Plague of God'; one of the 7 angels of punishment
Maktiel	This angel is in charge of trees
Malik	According to Arabic mythology this angel is associated with guarding the gates of hell
Malthidrelis	An angel of the sign of Aries
Maltiel	A Friday angel
Mameroijud	An angel of the 10th hour of the night
Mamiel	An angel of the 7th hour of the day
Mammon	A fallen angel

Manah	An angel of fertility
Manakel	An angel watcher of sea creatures and one of 72 angels of the zodiac
Maneij	An angel of the 4th hour of the night
Manuel	A ruling angel of the star sign of Cancer
Marchosias	A fallen angel
Marfiel	One of the angels of the 4th hour of the day
Margash	Also known as Archangel Metatron
Margiviel	An angel of the 4th heaven
Marifiel	An angel of the 8th hour of the night
Marioc	This angel watches over the writings of Enoch
Marmarath	One of the 7 planetary angels
Masgabriel	An angel of the 4th heaven who rules on Sundays
Masim	A guard of the gates of the East Wind
Maskriel	A guard of the 1st heaven
Maspiel	Angelic guard of the 2nd heaven
Matafiel	One of 7 guards of the 2nd heaven
Mataqiel	A guard of the 1st heaven
Matarel	Angel of rain

Mathiel	Ruler of Tuesdays who serves in 5th heaven
Mathlai	Wednesday angel and ruler of the planet Mercury; resides in the 3rd heaven
Mavet	An angel of death
Maymon	Saturday angel and a ruler of the Air
Mbriel	This angel rules the winds
Mebabel	A zodiac angel
Mechiel	A zodiac angel
Mediat	A Wednesday angel who watches over the planet Mercury; also known as King of the Angels
Medussusiel	An angel of the 6th hour of the day
Mefathiel	According to superstition this angel is an opener of doors
Mehahel	An angel of the order of the Cherubim
Mehaiah	An angel of the order of Principalities
Meher	This angel has special interest in justice
Mehiel	This angel protects authors, orators and university professors
Mehuman	One of 7 angels of confusion whose name means 'True, Faithful'
Meil	This angel has guardianship over Wednesdays
Melchisedec	An angel of the order of Virtues, sometimes identified as the Holy Ghost
Melech	An angel of the order of Powers

Meleyal	Whose name means 'Fullness of God'; an angel of Autumn
Melkejal	Also known as Machidel. An angel of March
Melkiel	An angel of the 4 seasons
Memsiel	One of the angels of the 7th hour of the night
Memuneh	Whose name means 'Appointed One'; a dispenser of dreams
Mephistopheles	Meaning 'He Who Loves Not the Light'
Meresijm	An angel of the 1st hour of the day
Meriarijm	A ruling angel of the night
Meros	One of the angels of the 9th hour of the day
Meshabber	Angel in charge of the death of animals, according to Rabbinic Lore
Mesriel	Angel of the 10th hour of the day
Metatron	'The angel of death,' whose role is to assist those crossing over to the other-side. One of the great archangels and said to be in charge of the sustenance of the world
Michael	Michael's name appears in Judaism, Christianity and Islam. His name means 'Who Is As God' and he is considered chief of the order of virtues and chief archangel
Midiel	A captain in the angelic army
Midrash	Also known as Metatron
Mihael	A ruling angel of fertility
Mikael	A governing angel of monarchs and noblemen

Mikhar	An angel with control over the waters of life
Mikhail	Mikhail resides in the 7th heaven. He is said to have not laughed once since hell was created. Mikhail is Arabic for Michael
Mikiel	One of the 72 angels of the Zodiac
Milkiel	Whose name means 'My Kingdom Is God'
Milliel	An angel with guardianship over Wednesdays
Mirael	One of the chiefs of the celestial armies
Missaln	An angel of the moon with guardianship over Mondays
Modiel	A guardian angel of the gates of the East Wind
Morael	An angel of fear who has the power to make things invisible
Moroni	The Mormon angel of God and considered the author of the final book in the *Book of Mormon* history
Mtniel	Ruler of tame beasts along with Jehiel and Hayyael
Mufjar	A guard of the 1st heaven
Mufliel	A guard of the 7th heaven
Mumiah	An angel of medicine and physics
Mupiel	Whose name means 'Out of the Mouth of God'
Murdad	An angel of July in Persian Lore
Muriel	Angel of June; ruler of the zodiac sign of Cancer
Murmur	A fallen angel

Naamah	Whose name means 'Pleasing'; an angel of prostitution
Nacoriel	Angel of the 9th hour of the night
Nadiel	An angel of December
Nafriel	A guard of the gates of the South Wind
Nahaliel	Whose name means 'Valley of God'; watches over streams
Nahuriel	A guard of the 1st heaven
Narcoriel	An angel of the 8th hour of the night
Narel	According to ancient lore an angel of Winter
Nathanael	Translates as 'Gift of God'; one of 12 angels of Vengeance and Lord of Fire
Ndmh	An angel of the Summer Equinox
Neciel	An angel watching over the 28 mansions of the moon
Negef	An angel of destruction
Nelapa	An angel of the 2nd heaven
Nemamiah	A guardian angel of generals and admirals
Neqael	A fallen archangel
Nestoriel	An angel of the 1st hour of the day

Nestozoz	An angel of the 3rd hour of the night
Nithael	A fallen angel
Nuriel	Whose name means 'Fire'; the angel of hailstones mentioned in Jewish legend

Och	According to some occultist groups this angel is an angel of the sun
Oertha	An angel of the North
Ofael	An angel of Tuesdays
Ol	A ruling angel over the zodiac sign of Leo
Onafiel	An angel of the moon according to Longfellow
Onoel	An alternative spelling for Haniel
Orael	An angel watcher of the planet Saturn
Oriares	A winter angel
Oriel	Another name for Auriel ('Light of God')
Ormael	An angel of the 4th hour of the night
Ormary	An angel of the 11th hour of the day
Ormas	An angel of the 10th hour of the day
Ormijel	An angel of the 4th hour of the day

Ormisiel	An angel of the 2nd hour of the night
Osael	Rules over Tuesdays
Osgaèbial	An angelic ruler of the 8th hour of the day

Pabel	One of the angels of the 4th heaven who watches over Sundays, the Lord's Day
Pachdiel	Whose name means 'Fear'; an angel guard of the 4th heaven
Pachriel	One of 7 angels appointed over the 7 Celestial Heavens
Padael	A guardian of the gates of the West Wind
Paffran	An angel of Tuesdays
Pahadiel	An angel of the 7th heaven
Pahadron	An angel of terror
Palpeltiyah	Another spelling of Archangel Metatron
Paltriel	A guardian of the 5th heaven
Pammon	This angel rules over the 6th hour of the night
Panael	A guardian of the gates of the North Wind
Pariukh	One of 2 guardian angels of the Enoch literature
Parziel	A guardian of the 6th heaven

Pasiel	A controlling angel of the star sign Pisces
Pasuy	A guardian of the 4th heaven
Patrozin	One of the angels of the 5th hour of the night
Pedael	Whose name means 'Whom God Delivers'; an angel of deliverance
Peliel	Chief of the Order of Virtues
Penac	One of the angels of the 3rd heaven
Penael	An angel of Fridays
Penarys	Angel of the 3rd hour of the night
Penat	One of many Friday angels
Penatiel	An angel of the 12th hour of the day
Pendros	An angel of the 7th hour of the night
Penemue	One of the fallen angels
Peniel	A Friday angel of the 3rd heaven
Periel	Also known as Metatron
Permaz	One of the angels of the 2nd hour of the night
Permiel	One of the angels of the 4th hour of the day
Pesagniyah	An angel with control of 'the keys of the ethereal spaces'
Pesak	A guardian angel stationed at the 5th heavenly hall

Phanuel	The archangel of penance and an angel of the Presence
Pharniel	Angel of the 12th hour of the day
Pharzuph	Angel of lust
Phatiel	Angel of the 5th hour of the night
Phorlakh	Angel of Earth
Phorsiel	Angel of the 4th hour of the night
Phul	A Monday angel and Lord of the Moon
Pihon	Another name for Metatron
Pilalael	A guardian angel of the gates of the West Wind
Porna	An angel of Fridays
Porosa	Another Friday angel
Pralimiel	Watches over the 11th hour of the day
Praxil	A ruling angel of the 2nd hour of the night
Prenostix	Watches over the 6th hour of the night
Pruel	A guard of the gates of the South Wind
Pruflas	A fallen angel
Purson	A fallen angel
Pusiel	An angel of punishment

Q

Qafshiel	One of the angels with charge over the Moon
Qalbam	One of many angelic guards of the gates of the South Wind
Qamiel	Another guard of the gates of the South Wind
Quelamia	A throne angel residing in the 1st heaven

R

Raamiel	Whose name means 'Trembling Before God'; an angel of thunder
Rael	According to some sources an angel ruling over Wednesdays and the planet Venus
Raguel	Whose name means 'Friend of God' is one of the archangels, in charge of good behaviour and an angel of Earth
Rahab	An angel of the sea also known as 'Sar Shel Yam' which means 'prince of the primordial sea'
Rahmiel	Angel of Mercy and an angel of Love
Rahtiel	'To Run'. In Jewish traditions is the angel of Constellations
Ramiel	Many believe that the name Ramiel, which is mentioned in Milton's *Paradise Lost* was in fact created by Milton (although this is not proven). Ramiel is the 'Chief of Thunder'. Also associated with visions
Rampel	An angel of mountain ranges and deep water

Raphael	Mentioned in the Bible, Raphael means 'God Has Healed' or 'Shining One'. Raphael is one of the traditional archangels
Raquiel	A guardian angel of the gates of the West Wind
Rashiel	Angel of whirlwinds and earthquakes
Rashu	An angel who stands at the bridge to heaven; 'a weigher of souls'
Raziel	Name means 'Secret of God'; angel of mysteries, and the author of the *Book of Raziel*, the book given to Adam
Razziel	An angel of the 7th hour of the night
Rehael	An angel of health who inspires parental respect
Remiel	A Throne angel
Requiel	One of 28 angels ruling the 28 mansions of the moon
Rhamiel	The angel name for St Francis of Assisi ('Angel of Mercy')
Rhaumel	An angel of Fridays
Rimezin	A ruling angel of the 4th hour of the night
Rochel	This angel helps to find lost objects
Rogziel	Whose name means 'Wrath of God'; an angel of punishment
Ruchiel	Angel of the Wind
Rudosor	Angel of the 6th hour of the night
Rumjal	One of many fallen angels
Rusvon	This angel is said to hold the keys to the Muslim paradise on Earth

S

Saaphiel	The angel of Hurricanes
Sabathiel	An angel of the planet Saturn
Sabrael	Some name Sabrael as one of the 7 archangels
Sachiel	Whose name means 'Covering of God'; depending on which reference you source he is an angel of Mondays, Thursdays or Fridays
Saelel	According to the Kabalah, one of 72 angels in control of the zodiac
Safkas	Another name for Metatron
Safriel	A guard of the 5th heaven
Sagiel	An angel of the 7th hour of the day
Sahaqiel	A ruler of the sky
Saissiel	An angel of the zodiac sign of Scorpio
Sakniel	One of the angels who guard the gates of the West Wind
Salmon	An angel of the 6th hour of the night
Samax	A ruling angel of the air and another Tuesday angel
Sameveel	A fallen angel
Samiel	Another spelling for Seir
Samil	An angel of the 6th hour

Sammael	Translates to 'Poison Angel'; an angel of good and bad. Some traditions list Sammael as an angel of death
Samuil	Whose name means 'Heard of God'; an Earth angel
Sandalphon	An archangel originally said to have been the human Elijah. Known as the twin brother of the archangel Metatron
Sangariah	The angel of Fasts
Santanael	An angel of Fridays
Sapiel	An angel of Sundays, the Lord's Day
Saraiel	A governor of the sign of Gemini
Sariel	One of the 7 archangels. Various other names include the spelling Suriel and Saraqel. Name means 'God's Command'. Occasionally identified as archangel Uriel
Sarquamich	An angel of the 3rd hour of the night
Satael	A Tuesday angel
Satan	Traditionally the fallen angel associated with evil, after he was said to have led a revolt against God
Saturn	An angel of the Wilderness
Sauriel	An angel of Death
Sedekiah	An angel who finds treasure
Seeliah	A fallen angel, who had (or maybe still has) control over vegetables
Sefriel	A guard of the 5th heaven

Seheiah	This angel provides protection
Sehibiel	A guard of the 2nd heaven
Seir	Another spelling for Samiel
Semanglaf	This angel helps with pregnancy
Semyaza	Leader of the fallen angels
Seraf	An angel of fire
Serapiel	An angel of the 5th hour of the day
Seraqel	A guardian of fruit-bearing trees
Serviel	Angel of the 3rd hour of the day
Shadfiel	A guardian angel of the North Wind
Shahrivar	According to ancient Persian Lore this is angel of August
Shakziel	An angel of water insects
Shalgiel	An angel of snow
Shastaniel	A guardian of the gates of the South Wind
Shekiniel	An angel of the 4th heaven
Shelemial	A guardian of the 3rd heaven
Shimshiel	A guardian of the gates of the East Wind
Shlomiel	A guard of the 3rd heaven
Shoftiel	Whose name means 'Judge of God'; one of 7 angels of punishment

Shosoriyah	Also known as Metatron
Shriniel	A guardian angel of the 4th heaven
Sila	An angel of Power
Simapesiel	A fallen angel
Sizajasel	An angel of the star sign Sagitarius
Sizouze	An angel of prayers
Sofiel	An angel of fruit & vegetables
Sofriel	An angel record keeper
Somcham	A guardian angel of the gates of the West Wind
Soncas	Another Tuesday angel
Sonneillon	A fallen angel
Sophia	Name means 'Wisdom'; also known as Pistis Sophia
Splenditenes	This angel is said to support the heavens on his back
Spugliguel	An angel of Spring
Ssakmakiel	One of the angels of the star sign Aquarius
Sturbiel	An angel of the 4th hour of the day
Sui'el	An angel of earthquakes
Sumiel	One of the leaders of the fallen angels
Suriel	Often named as one of the great archangels, name means 'God's Command'

Tabkiel	Another name for archangel Metatron
Tagriel	An angel ruling one of the 28 mansions of the Moon
Taliahad	An angel of water
Tamael	According to tradition an angel of Friday
Tamarid	An angel of the 2nd hour of the night
Tarfaniel	A guardian angel of the gates of the West Wind
Tariel	An angel of Summer
Tarniel	One of many angels of Wednesdays
Tarquam	An angel of Autumn
Tarwan	One of several angels accompanying the Sun each day
Tatriel	One of many names for the Archangel Metatron
Tebliel	An angel of the Earth
Tehom	A Throne angel
Tehoriel	An angel guard of the gates of the South Wind
Temeluch	This angel watches over childbirth and looks after young children
Tempast	One of the angels of the 1st hour of the night

Tempha	An angel of the planet Saturn
Tenaciel	One of many angels of Friday
Teriapel	A ruling angel of the planet Venus
Tezalel	An angel of fidelity
Thiel	One of many angels of Wednesday
Thomax	One of the angels of the 8th hour of the night
Tiel	A guardian angel of the gates of the North Wind
Tir	An angel of the month of June
Tiriel	A ruling angel of the planet Mercury
Tirtael	One of the many guardians of the gates of the East Wind
Todatamael	Another guardian of the gates of the East Wind
Tophtharthareth	One of the angels of the planet Mercury
Torquaret	An angel of the season of Autumn
Tsadkiel	An angel of the planet Jupiter
Tual	Ruling over the sign of Taurus
Tubiel	An angel of Summer
Tufiel	A guardian of the 1st heaven
Tufriel	An angel guard of the 6th heaven
Tumoriel	An angel of the 11th hour of the night

Turmiel	An angel guard of the gates of the West Wind
Tzadiqel	An archangel dedicated to Thursdays and the planet Jupiter
Tzarmiel	An angel guard of the gates of the North Wind
Tzurel	A guardian of the gates of the South Wind

U

Ubaviel	An angel of the sign of Capricorn
Ucirmiel	A Wednesday angel
Umabel	This angel has control over Astronomy and Physics
Umahel	According to some sources an Archangel
Urian	Also known as Uriel
Uriel	'God is Fire' or 'Fire of God'. One of the leading archangels. Sometimes called a seraph or a cherub. He is said to stand at the Gate of Eden with his fiery sword. Presides over thunder and terror
Urjan	Another name for Uriel
Uryan	Another spelling for Uriel
Urzla	An angel of the East
Usiel	Usiel, whose name means 'Strength of God', is thought to be a fallen angel
Uvabriel	An angel of the 3rd hour of the night

Uvael	A Monday angel
Uvall	A fallen angel
Uvayah	Also known as Archangel Metatron
Uwula	An angel called upon during eclipses of the Sun or Moon

Vacabiel	A ruler of the star sign Pisces
Vachmiel	An angel of the 4th hour of the day
Valnum	An angel of Mondays
Varcan	A controlling angel of the Sun
Veguaniel	An angel of the 3rd hour of the day
Vehofnehu	Another name for Metatron
Vel	An angel of Wednesdays
Vel Aquiel	An angel of Sundays
Venahel	A Wednesday angel
Verchiel	An angel of July and ruler of the sign of Leo
Vetuel	An angel of Mondays
Vianuel	A Tuesday angel
Vngsursh	Angel of the Summer Equinox

Vocasiel	Ruling the zodiac sign of Pisces
Voel	An angel of the sign of Virgo
Voizia	An angel of the 12th hour of the day
Vraniel	An angel of the 10th hour of the night
Vretil	An angel record keeper
Vrihaspati	This angel watches over hymns and prayers
Vvael	An angel of Mondays

W

Wallim	An angel resident in the 1st heaven

Y

Yahala	A guardian angel of the gates of the West Wind
Yahanaq Rabba	An angel of the gates of the East Wind
Yahriel	An angel of the Moon
Yahsiyah	Another spelling Archangel Metatron
Yekahel	A ruling angel of the planet Mercury
Yeliel	A guardian angel of the gates of the South Wind
Yonel	An angel guardian of the gates of the North Wind

Yrouel An angel of Fear

Yurkemi An angel of Hail

Za'afiel Whose name means 'Wrath of God'; an angel of hurricanes

Zacharael 'Remembrance of God'; according to some sources one of the 7 archangels

Zacharel An angel of the 7th hour of the night

Zachriel An angel of Memory

Zadakiel A ruling angel of the planet Jupiter

Zadkiel The angel of Jupiter and the angel of benevolence. Zadkiel means 'The Righteousness of God' and is one of the seven archangels according to some traditions

Zakkiel An angel of Storms

Zaliel An angel of Tuesdays

Zaniel A ruling angel of the star sign Libra

Zanziel An angel guardian of the gates of the West Wind

Zaphkiel 'Knowledge of God'; listed as one of the 7 archangels

Zavael An angel controlling whirlwinds

Zazahiel An angel of the 3rd heaven

Zazriel	'Strength of God'; an angel of power and strength
Zebuleon	This angel is said to be one of the judges at the end of the world
Zechariel	Whose name means 'Jehovah Remembers'; an angel of the planet Jupiter
Zeruch	An angel of strength
Zethar	An angel of confusion
Zobiachel	An angel ruling the planet Jupiter. (The name only appears to be found in the works of Longfellow)
Zoigmiel	An angel of the 9th hour of the day
Zuriel	An angel of the sign of Libra

4

Angel Names and Their Meanings

Angel Names and Their Meanings

*'And within each light of God's perfect flame,
Lies an angel by any other name…'*

ANON

Really, despite the long list given in the A–Z previously, angels don't have names at all! As a race, humankind has designated the names of the angels. Many of these names appear in religious texts and historical documents, and traditionally the names relate to the angels' roles and the fact that they work through the Divine Source (God).

Angel names in current use nearly all end in the suffix '*-el*' or '*-il*', which is Hebrew for '*of the Lord*'. Or they can end in '*-elf*' (Old English), '*-aelf*' (Anglo-Saxon), '*-ellu*' (Welsh) or '*-aillil*' (Irish), meaning '*shining one*' or '*radiant being*'.

The combination makes up the name and role of the angels.

'*Arch*' – the prefix of the word Archangel, means principal. So, archangel literally translates as 'principal angel' or 'the angel in charge'. Some sources confuse Ariel and Uriel, while others list the various spellings as separate angels.

ARCHANGEL NAMES

ARCHANGEL NAME	MEANINGS/TRANSLATIONS
Adabiel	This may be another name for Abdiel, meaning 'Servant of God'
Ariel	'Lion' or 'Lioness of God', 'Earth's Great Lord', 'Shining Earth'
Azrael	'Whom God Helps'
Chamuel	'He who Sees God', 'He who Seeks God'
Gabriel	'God is my Strength', 'Governor of Light', 'Man of God', 'Power of God'. Gabriel is called the Angel of Truth
Haniel	'Glory of God', 'Grace of God'. Known as the Angel of Love and Harmony
Jeremiel	'Mercy of God'
Jophiel	'Beauty of God'
Metatron	Because Metatron's name does not have the traditional ending, the meaning of his name is unclear. Suggested meanings include 'Angel of the Presence' and 'Sitting Next to the Throne of the Divine'. Many call him the 'Greatest of all the Angels'
Michael	'He who is Like God', 'Looks Like God'. Michael is known as The Great Protector
Raguel	'Friend of God'
Raphael	'God Heals', 'God has Healed', 'Angel of the Sun', 'Angel of the East', 'Shining Healer'. Known as the Angel of Love
Raziel	'Secret of God', 'Angel of Mysteries', 'Prince of Knowledge'
Sandalphon	As with Metatron, there is no traditional meaning for this name, although he is often called the Prince of Prayers
Uriel	'Light of God', 'Fire of God'
Zadkiel	'Righteousness of God'. Called The Brilliant One

Some references indicate that the names do not relate to individual angels at all and might, in fact, refer to whole hosts of angels.

Angels who work with humans may indicate a name by which they may be called, or you can create a name that feels right to you. This name can be either male or female or one that refers to both aspects.

ANGEL NAMES IN TRANSLATION

Many translations for the name 'Angel' literally translate as messenger or courier. In the earliest of Christian times, 'daimon' (demon) and the word 'angel' are almost interchangeable.

ANGEL	TRANSLATED INTO OTHER LANGUAGES/RELIGIONS
Albanian	engjëll
Belarusan	aniol
Bulgarian	àíãåë
Cebuano	anghel
Croatian	andjeo
Czech	andel
Danish	engel
Dutch	engel
English	angel
Esperanto	ang^elo
Estonian	ingel
Filipino	anghel
Finnish	enkeli
French	ange
German	engel
Greek	άγγελος
Greek (ancient)	a[ggeloß
Hawaiian	'anela
Hungarian	angyal
Icelandic	engill
Ilongo	orasyon
Italian	angelo
Indonesian/Malayian	malaikat
Latin	angelus
Latin American Spanish	ángel
Latvian	eņgelis
Maori	anahera
Norwegian	engle
Polish	anielski
Portuguese	anjo
Romanian	înger
Russian	ангел
Serbian	andeo
Serbo-Croatian	anđeoski
Slovak	anjel
Spanish	angel
Swedish	ängel
Turkish	melek
Yiddish	malach
Welsh	angyles

5

The Angelic Hierarchy

The Angelic Hierarchy

*G*iven our human instinct for classification and organization, it was only a matter of time before we classified our spiritual guardians. The gap between God and man was seen as too large and it seemed only natural that there would be a chain of command. At the lower level, we have 'Angels', a name often used to signify a 'guardian angel' as well as the collective term for all of our celestial helpers. The angels work most closely with humankind and the Earth. At the upper level are the 'Seraphim', whose role is to sing the praises of God, a role thought to possibly help with lifting the energy of the divine.

ST THOMAS AQUINAS

One of the earliest people to make this classification was the philosopher Thomas Aquinas (1225–1274). Thomas was a philosopher and Catholic theologian, born in a place called Roccasecca, near Aquina in Italy. He was sent to study at the famous Benedictine monastery in Monte Cassino when he was only six years old.

Later he was made a teacher and, in 1257, a lecturer of theology. For several years he taught Bible studies. Thomas was very much devoted to prayer and to the life of his religious order, and spent many hours writing biblical commentaries and a series on the work of Aristotle, by whose ideas he was very influenced. One of his most famous works is the collection of reflection pieces he wrote about angels and the celestial framework he recorded – the *Summa Theologiae*. He was canonized in 1323 and named *Doctor Angelicus* of the church by Pius X in 1567. He was also acknowledged as the patron saint of Catholic schools in 1880.

He never finished his *Summa Theologiae* (a three-part treatise on sacred doctrine), which discussed the creation, human nature, God and the angels. However Thomas demonstrates that angels are pure spirits created by God, and to disregard them destroys the very balance of the universe – the perfection of the universe demanding that these intellectual creatures exist, created by God's intelligence and by God's will. He thought of angels very much as incorporeal (without bodies), existing as spiritual energy (which deviated from work by earlier philosophers who believed angels might be made from a material substance), although they could, on occasion, take on a physical body if required.

Thomas also stated that even supposed 'fallen' angels like Lucifer, as with all angels, were created as perfect and pure beings, but may have exercised 'free will'. He believed that angels could only be in one place at one time, but that they had the ability to 'travel' instantly from one place to another in a way that does not have any meaning within our understanding of time as we know it. Thomas believed that angels have free will (a point not agreed upon by everyone), being free to love God. They are not capable of committing sin themselves (apart from the sins of pride and envy), but are guilty of leading humankind to commit sin.

Angels communicate by sending thoughts to each other. Words are not used. They consult God by contemplating him. The higher-level angels (those closer to God) can enlighten the angels at the lower levels but cannot influence their free will. Thomas also agreed with St Jerome (following Matthew 18:10) that each human has his or her own guardian angel, a role played by the 9th order of angels, known simply as 'angels'.

THE TRIADIC HIERARCHY

For thousands of years the angels have been split into three distinct levels and, within each, three more levels or classes of angels. Each section is given different roles and tasks and each has its own ruling angels.

Variations exist between the names of these levels depending on the different sources and authorities. One of the most used versions of the angelic hierarchy is that of Pseudo-Dionysius, which is also recognized by the great Thomas Aquinas.

The higher levels of angels are those closest to God and the lower levels are nearer to humankind. The angelic hierarchy does help the human mind to bridge the gap between God and us – an impossible concept to imagine otherwise.

When you search into the many angel names associated with each level you often find angels appear on several of the levels. They seem to move up and down the chain of command as required (the archangels in particular).

Angelic Order	Role	Sphere/Triad
1. Seraphim	The Seraphim have the role of lifting the energy of the God essence. They are said to sit each side of the Lord, singing his praises.	The 1st sphere/triad. Working closest with God
2. Cherubim	Cherubim work with the higher levels of Universal energy, concerning themselves with the stars and the sun. Powerful and 'awe-inspiring', with four faces and four wings.	
3. Thrones	This level of angels work with divine judgement. The thrones are also known as 'Wheels' or 'the ones with many eyes'.	
4. Dominions/ Dominations	Dominions work directly with the lower levels of angels, passing messages down through the hierarchy, controlling the order of the cosmos.	The 2nd sphere/triad. Each assigned with a specific planet and working with the angelic levels below them
5. Virtues	The Virtues work on a higher planetary level, preceding over the elements and watching over every detail of nature.	
6. Powers	This section includes the angels with control over the living and dying.	
7. Princes/ Principalities	Principalities have control over cities and nations and bigger groups of people including towns, cities and districts.	The 3rd sphere/triad. Working as celestial messengers and guardians, working closest to humankind
8. Archangels	We are familiar with many of the archangels, including Archangel Michael and Archangel Gabriel. Often there are mentioned 'The 7 archangels', with each religion and tradition suggesting variations on this named list!	
9. Angels	As well as 'angels' being a collective term for all the celestial beings, the name 'Angel' also indicates those angels we also call 'Guardian Angels', or those closest to humankind and responsible for each living being.	

SO WHAT ARE CHERUBS?

Traditional artwork depicts cherubs as chubby babies with wings. Yet the word 'cherub' comes from the word 'cherubim', and the cherubim are one of the nine choirs or orders of angels. The cherubim are actually magnificent and powerful assistants of the Almighty!

The Cherubim are guardians of the light and the stars, and part of the first Sphere of angels. They sit just below the Seraphim in terms of power and closeness to the Divine. The Cherubim are wise and knowledgeable. They are the keepers of the heavenly records and guard the gates of Heaven.

The earliest statues of the Cherubim show them as beings with human faces and the bodies of bulls and lions. Some ancient references depict them as having four wings and four faces. The Hebrews called them the Kerub, which may translate to 'one who intercedes'.

6

Archangels

Archangels

THE TRADITIONAL ROLES OF
THE ARCHANGELS

Some angels are well known to us, in particular those mentioned in religious texts, fables and legions. There is almost an 'Archangel Top 10', although there are many more archangels than these. The reason we know about this select group is that they are the protectors of the planet Earth. Other realms and planets have their own archangels.

According to *The Hierarchy of the Blessed Angels* (Thomas Heywood 1635) the Archangels Gabriel, Michael, Raphael and Uriel have particular authority and guardianship over the planet earth. Jewish traditions suggest there are seven archangels with this role: Admael, Arciciah, Ariel, Tabbashael, Azriel, Arhiel and Horabael.

'Every visible thing in this world is put in charge of an angel.'

SAINT AUGUSTINE

HOW MANY ARCHANGELS ARE THERE?

The archangels are said to be a separate choir in the order of angels (or angel hierarchy), but they are also said to stand above many of the other ranks. Sometimes they appear to be part of many different levels, or perhaps they are able to move up and down through the ranks.

The most important of these archangels (traditionally numbered as seven) fulfil many different roles and are often called 'The Princes of the Seven Heavens'. The Third Book of Enoch says that these archangels are each attended by 496,000 myriads of ministering angels. (A myriad denotes vast numbers of angels or sometimes 'ten thousand'.) This number is also supported in Revelations (8:2) and the book of Tobit (12:15).

You have probably heard of Archangel Michael and Archangel Gabriel, but who are the other archangels? Michael, Gabriel, Raphael and Ariel (or Uriel – some list Ariel and Uriel as one angel and other sources suggest that they are two different beings) appear in many sources. Other suggestions include Raguel, Zadkiel, Metatron, Sandalphon and others.

Islam recognizes four archangels (Asrael, Gabriel, Israfel and Michael), although some sources say twelve! However, the Koran names only two – Djibril (Gabriel) and Michael.

In some of the tables of information relating to the archangels, we have included a smaller number, because we are unaware of all the talents and skills of the less well-known archangels.

WHAT ARE THE NAMES OF THE ARCHANGELS

As you will see by the many references to the archangels in this book, it is almost impossible to clarify! Here are the most commonly mentioned archangels (with the names taken from places such as the Bible, the First Book of Enoch, the Koran and the list of Dionysius the Areopagite).

Archangel Ariel – Overseer of Nature

Archangel Ariel is often confused with Archangel Uriel. Ariel is said to work with Raphael in healing the animals of the world, and watches over wild animals, fish and birds. He looks over the fairy kingdoms and nature spirits and keeps water clean and pure.

Ariel is often called in divine magic and spirit releasement. He is usually associated with Lions and is said to have the head of a lion. Ariel is usually pictured carrying a scroll.

Archangel Azrael – Angel of Death

Azrael is saddled with the unpleasant title the 'Angel of Death', and as foreboding as it sounds, the title indicates his role as the recorder of life and death. His appearance is said to be particularly unpleasant, with as many eyes and tongues as there are people upon the earth, and 4,000 wings. I can imagine that he would appear very scary!

Azrael is called upon by fishermen of the world, and is associated with water and 'going with the flow'. He also helps with blockages of a spiritual nature.

Archangel Chamuel – Gatekeeper to the World

Archangel Chamuel is in charge of world peace, and is very concerned with protection. He is like an angelic bouncer! Like Archangel Michael, Chamuel is a warrior who represents justice.

He has another side and some see him as a loving, kind and gentle angel who helps to recover lost items, helps us to find our soul mates and is concerned with such things as beauty, joy and happiness.

Archangel Gabriel – Heavenly Communicator

Gabriel is another of the top-ranking angels and is best known for communication skills, being the messenger who brought the word of the impending birth of Jesus to the Virgin Mary. Gabriel is usually shown holding a lily, with an inkwell and pen and dressed in blue.

Many see Gabriel as a female angel or an angel of feminine energy and one who sits to the left-hand side of the Lord. Gabriel is known as the angel who dictated the Koran to Mohammed. Gabriel is known as 'Djibril' in Arabic.

Archangel Haniel – Angel of the Moon

Haniel is usually credited with the role of Chief of the orders of Principalities and Virtues, and is most well known for escorting Enoch to the spiritual realms.

Haniel is sometimes given feminine qualities and is said to be associated with the moon and strong psychic and mystical energies. She recovers lost healing secrets and harnesses the moon's energy in crystals and potions relating to healing and health.

Archangel Jeremiel – Overseer of Souls

Jeremiel is the angel who looks after souls waiting to reincarnate, dealing with 'past life reviews' in particular. Whilst souls are in their earthly bodies, he helps with psychic dreams and clairvoyance.

In Judaic texts he is named as one of the seven archangels. His energy is said to be kind, loving, protective and compassionate. He is called to help with life changes.

Archangel Jophiel – Angel of Paradise

Jophiel is the Prince of the angelic choir of the order of Cherubim and another angel who is associated with feminine energy. Jophiel is most famous for watching over Noah's sons.

Call Jophiel if you are working in creative endeavours. Jophiel inspires creative thought, and helps you to find your inner light and move forward on your spiritual path.

Archangel Metatron – Angel of the Presence

Metatron (formerly the human Enoch) is the keeper of the Akashic Records (the Book of Life). He is the first angel who was created from a human being (and the twin of Sandalphon).To many he is the most powerful of all the archangels.

If you need help with relationships, careers, children and spiritual gifts, then Metatron can help you. He is usually pictured in luxurious clothing and holding a pen and book.

Archangel Michael – Commander in Chief of the Heavenly Armies

Michael is the most well known of all the Archangels and the one that appears most regularly (he is included in the Christian, Judaic and Islamic faiths). He is usually pictured with his flaming sword and shown as a handsome, strong and powerful male angel. He is sometimes pictured as a slayer of dragons.

His primary role is of protector and he is the angel of Judgment Day. In Islam he is 'Mikhail' and is called St Michael by the Christians. One of his roles is said to be the 'weigher of souls'.

Archangel Raguel – Angel of Earth

Raguel is one of the seven archangels who are listed in the great *Book of Enoch*. One of his roles is to keep other angels in order. Raguel is most well known for his role in lifting Enoch (the human made into an angel) up to heaven, and is usually placed in the order of the Principalities.

Raguel is primarily involved with resolving disagreements and creating harmony. He acts as a defender of the people and has 'empowering' qualities. He is the archangel of fairness and justice.

Archangel Raphael – Guardian of the Tree of Life/Divine Healer

Raphael is best known for his work as a healer. He is usually pictured walking with a staff or caduceus entwined with a snake. He has his right forefinger pointing toward heaven (a sign of encouragement and hope).

Raphael works closely with healers, health professionals and therapists. Raphael is also the patron of travellers.

Archangel Raziel – Angel of Mysteries

Archangel Raziel works closely with the creator. He has understanding of all the higher sciences like quantum physics and sacred geometry, and is associated with serious levels of psychic study, magical abilities and esoteric materials.

He is most well known for *The Book of Raziel*, which is said to contain the secrets of the universe. He handed Adam the book of guidance after Adam was evicted from the Garden of Eden (these secrets were also given to Enoch before his ascension).

Archangel Sandalphon – The Tall Angel/Prayer Gatherer

Archangel Sandalphon (formerly the human prophet Elijah) is known as one of the tallest angels in heaven and said to be the twin brother (or twin flame) of Metatron. Like the human Enoch, Sandalphon was lifted to the heavens and made into an angel for his good works as a human man whilst on the earth. He was lifted up into heaven by a fiery chariot pulled by two horses (recorded in 2 Kings in the Bible).

His role is to carry the prayers of humans up to God, and he helps with unborn babies and protecting the unborn child.

Archangel Sariel – Presiding Angel of the Sun/Prince of Presence

Archangel Sariel is a lesser known 'watcher angel', or one who 'keeps watch', and has been given guardianship of the spirits of 'children' of humankind and angels who have sinned whilst in the heavenly realms (apparently!). Sariel is also in the unfortunate position of being known as a fallen angel according to some traditions, although recognized as an angel of healing in others.

Sariel has guardianship of the path of the Moon and is said to be a teacher of that knowledge. This was once undisclosed information of a secret nature.

Archangel Uriel – Angel of the Presence/Regent of the Sun

Uriel works most closely with the Earth and earth healing. He is the angel who orchestrates transformation of the planet following natural disasters such as floods, fires and earthquakes. God sent Uriel to Noah to warn him of the Flood.

Traditionally, Uriel is the angel who is credited with giving Adam a book of medicinal herbs and is said to have the power of manifestation.

Archangel Zadkiel – Archangel of Mercy and Benevolence

Zadkiel helps you to feel forgiveness and kindness towards yourself and others. Archangel Zadkiel is said to be one of the most gentle of archangels and has the energy of comfort and prayer.

He is a Throne angel (standing in the presence of God), and is most famous for stopping Abraham from sacrificing his son Isaac as an offering to God.

ARCHANGEL NAMES/VARIATIONS CROSS-REFERENCED

Names have varied with each religion and culture and many changes to spellings have occurred around the world. The following list will help with which archangel is which. You can see with the similarity between spellings of similar angels how people get confused between the names! It took weeks of research to create this list with names being added and sometimes deleted along the way.

Just when I thought I had the list completed another name would appear, only to never be seen anywhere else!

NAME	ALSO KNOWN AS
Abdiel	Adabriel; Adabiel; Arcade
Abruel	Gabriel; Jibril; Jiburili; Serafili
Abruel	Gabriel; Jibril (Muslim); Jiburili; Serafili; Jibraiil; Djibril; Gavriel; Jibra'il; Cambiel
Adabiel	Abdiel; Adabriel; Arcade
Adabriel	Abdiel; Adabiel; Arcade
Akrasiel	Raguel; Raguil; Rasuil; Rufael; Suryan
Anael	Haniel; Aniel; Hamiel; Omoel; Hamael; Hanael
Aniel	Haniel; Anael; Hamiel; Omoel; Hamael; Hanael
Arael	Ariel; Ariael; Ariella

Name	Also Known As
Arcade	Abdiel; Adabriel; Adabiel
Ariael	Arael; Ariel; Ariella
Ariel	Arael; Ariael; Ariella
Ariella	Ariel; Arael; Ariael
Asariel	Azrael; Azrail; Ashriel; Azriel; Azaril (also seen as Raphael)
Ashriel	Azrael; Azrail; Azriel; Azaril (also seen as Raphael); Asariel
Azaril (also seen as Raphael)	Azrael; Azrail; Ashriel; Azriel; Asariel
Azrael	Azrail; Ashriel; Azriel; Azaril (also seen as Raphael); Asariel
Azrail	Azrael; Ashriel; Azriel; Azaril (also seen as Raphael); Asariel
Azriel	Azrael; Azrail; Ashriel; Azaril (also seen as Raphael); Asariel
Beshter	Michael; Mika'il; Sabbathiel; St Michael
Camael	Chamuel; Camiel; Camiul; Camniel; Cancel; Jahoel; Kemuel; Khamael; Seraphiel; Shemuel; Shemael; Qemuel
Cambiel	Gabriel; Abruel; Jibril (Muslim); Jiburili; Serafili; Jibraiil; Djibril; Gavriel; Jibra'il
Camiel	Chamuel; Camael; Camiul; Camniel; Cancel; Jahoel; Kemuel; Khamael; Seraphiel; Shemuel; Shemael; Qemuel
Camiul	Chamuel; Camael; Camiel; Camniel; Cancel; Jahoel; Kemuel; Khamael; Seraphiel; Shemuel; Shemael; Qemuel
Camniel	Chamuel; Camael; Camiel; Camiul; Cancel; Jahoel; Kemuel; Khamael; Seraphiel; Shemuel; Shemael; Qemuel
Cancel	Chamuel; Camael; Camiel; Camiul; Camniel; Jahoel; Kemuel; Khamael; Seraphiel; Shemuel; Shemael; Qemuel
Chamuel	Camael; Camiel; Camiul; Camniel; Cancel; Jahoel; Kemuel; Khamael; Seraphiel; Shemuel; Shemael; Qemuel
Djibril	Gabriel; Abruel; Jibril (Muslim); Jiburili; Serafili; Jibraiil; Gavriel; Jibra'il; Cambiel
Gabriel	Abruel; Jibril; Jiburili; Serafili
Gabriel	Abruel; Jibril (Muslim); Jiburili; Serafili; Jibraiil; Djibril; Gavriel; Jibra'il; Cambiel
Gavriel	Gabriel; Abruel; Jibril (Muslim); Jiburili; Serafili; Jibraiil; Djibril; Jibra'il; Cambiel
Hamael	Haniel; Anael; Aniel; Hamiel; Omoel; Hanael

NAME	ALSO KNOWN AS
Hamiel	Haniel; Anael; Aniel; Omoel; Hamael; Hanael
Hanael	Haniel; Anael; Aniel; Hamiel; Omoel; Hamael
Haniel	Anael; Aniel; Hamiel; Omoel; Hamael; Hanael
Iofiel	Jophiel; Iophiel; Jofiel; Zophiel
Iophiel	Jophiel; Iofiel; Jofiel; Zophiel
Jahoel	Chamuel; Camael; Camiel; Camiul; Camniel; Cancel; Kemuel; Khamael; Seraphiel; Shemuel; Shemael; Qemuel
Jeremiel	Ramiel (also seen as Raphael); Remiel; Rhamiel; Ramaela
Jibraiil	Gabriel; Abruel; Jibril (Muslim); Jiburili; Serafili; Djibril; Gavriel; Jibra'il; Cambiel
Jibra'il	Gabriel; Abruel; Jibril (Muslim); Jiburili; Serafili; Jibraiil; Djibril; Gavriel; Cambiel
Jibril	Gabriel; Abruel; Jiburili; Serafili
Jibril (Muslim)	Gabriel; Abruel; Jiburili; Serafili; Jibraiil; Djibril; Gavriel; Jibra'il; Cambiel
Jiburili	Gabriel; Abruel; Jibril; Serafili
Jiburili	Gabriel; Abruel; Jibril (Muslim); Serafili; Jibraiil; Djibril; Gavriel; Jibra'il; Cambiel
Jofiel	Jophiel; Iofiel; Iophiel; Zophiel
Jophiel	Iofiel; Iophiel; Jofiel; Zophiel
Kemuel	Chamuel; Camael; Camiel; Camiul; Camniel; Cancel; Jahoel; Khamael; Seraphiel; Shemuel; Shemael; Qemuel
Khamael	Chamuel; Camael; Camiel; Camiul; Camniel; Cancel; Jahoel; Kemuel; Seraphiel; Shemuel; Shemael; Qemuel
Labbiel	Raphael; Ramiel (also seen as Jeremiel; Azrael); Tzaphiel
Meditron	Metatron (human name, Enoch); Shekinah; Metatetron; Merraton; Metaraon; Mittron; Metataon
Merraton	Metatron (human name, Enoch); Shekinah; Metatetron; Metaraon; Mittron; Metataon; Meditron
Metaraon	Metatron (human name, Enoch); Shekinah; Metatetron; Merraton; Mittron; Metataon; Meditron
Metataon	Metatron (human name, Enoch); Shekinah; Metatetron; Merraton; Metaraon; Mittron; Meditron

NAME	ALSO KNOWN AS
Metatetron	Metatron (human name, Enoch); Shekinah; Merraton; Metaraon; Mittron; Metataon; Meditron
Metatron (human name, Enoch)	Shekinah; Metatetron; Merraton; Metaraon; Mittron; Metataon; Meditron
Michael	Beshter; Mika'il; Sabbathiel; St Michael
Mika'il	Michael; Beshter; Sabbathiel; St Michael
Mittron	Metatron (human name, Enoch); Shekinah; Metatetron; Merraton; Metaraon; Metataon; Meditron
Omoel	Haniel; Anael; Aniel; Hamiel; Hamael; Hanael
Qemuel	Chamuel; Camael; Camiel; Camiul; Camniel; Cancel; Jahoel; Kemuel; Khamael; Seraphiel; Shemuel; Shemael
Raguel	Akrasiel; Raguil; Rasuil; Rufael; Suryan
Raguil	Raguel; Akrasiel; Rasuil; Rufael; Suryan
Ramaela	Jeremiel; Ramiel (also seen as Raphael); Remiel; Rhamiel
Ramiel (also seen as Jeremiel and Azrael)	Raphael; Labbiel; Tzaphiel
Ramiel (also seen as Raphael)	Jeremiel; Remiel; Rhamiel; Ramaela
Raphael	Labbiel; Ramiel (also seen as Jeremiel and Azrael) Tzaphiel;
Rasuil	Raguel; Akrasiel; Raguil; Rufael; Suryan
Ratziel	Raziel; Suriel; Suruel; Suriyel
Raziel	Ratziel; Suriel; Suruel; Suriyel
Remiel	Jeremiel; Ramiel (also seen as Raphael); Rhamiel; Ramaela
Rhamiel	Jeremiel; Ramiel (also seen as Raphael); Remiel; Ramaela
Rufael	Raguel; Akrasiel; Raguil; Rasuil; Suryan
Sabbathiel	Michael; Beshter; Mika'il; St Michael
Sahaqiel	Sariel; Sarakiel; Saraguel; Saraqael; Saraqel; Zerachiel
Sandalphon (human name, Elijah)	Sandolphon; Sandolfon
Sandolfon	Sandalphon (human name, Elijah); Sandolphon
Sandolphon	Sandalphon (human name, Elijah); Sandolfon
Saraguel	Sariel; Sarakiel; Saraqael; Saraqel; Zerachiel; Sahaqiel
Sarakiel	Sariel; Saraguel; Saraqael; Saraqel; Zerachiel; Sahaqiel

NAME	ALSO KNOWN AS
Saraqael	Sariel; Sarakiel; Saraguel; Saraqel; Zerachiel; Sahaqiel
Saraqel	Sariel; Sarakiel; Saraguel; Saraqael; Zerachiel; Sahaqiel
Sariel	Sarakiel; Saraguel; Saraqael; Saraqel; Zerachiel; Sahaqiel
Satqiel	Zadkiel; Tzadkiel; Zadakiel; Zidekiel
Satqiel	Zadkiel; Tzadkiel; Zadakiel; Zidekiel; Tzadiqel; Tsadkiel; Zachiel
Serafili	Gabriel; Abruel; Jibril; Jiburili
Serafili	Gabriel; Abruel; Jibril (Muslim); Jiburili; Jibraiil; Djibril; Gavriel; Jibra'il; Cambiel
Seraphiel	Chamuel; Camael; Camiel; Camiul; Camniel; Cancel; Jahoel; Kemuel; Khamael; Shemuel; Shemael; Qemuel
Shekinah	Metatron (human name, Enoch); Metatetron; Merraton; Metaraon; Mittron; Metataon; Meditron
Shemael	Chamuel; Camael; Camiel; Camiul; Camniel; Cancel; Jahoel; Kemuel; Khamael; Seraphiel; Shemuel; Qemuel
Shemuel	Chamuel; Camael; Camiel; Camiul; Camniel; Cancel; Jahoel; Kemuel; Khamael; Seraphiel; Shemael; Qemuel
St Michael	Michael; Beshter; Mika'il; Sabbathiel
Suriel	Raziel; Ratziel; Suruel; Suriyel
Suriyel	Raziel; Ratziel; Suriel; Suruel
Suruel	Raziel; Ratziel; Suriel; Suriyel
Suryan	Raguel; Akrasiel; Raguil; Rasuil; Rufael
Tsadkiel	Zadkiel; Satqiel; Tzadkiel; Zadakiel; Zidekiel; Tzadiqel; Zachiel
Tzadiqel	Zadkiel; Satqiel; Tzadkiel; Zadakiel; Zidekiel; Tsadkiel; Zachiel
Tzadkiel	Zadkiel; Satqiel; Zadakiel; Zidekiel
Tzadkiel	Zadkiel; Satqiel; Zadakiel; Zidekiel; Tzadiqel; Tsadkiel; Zachiel
Tzaphiel	Raphael; Labbiel; Ramiel (also seen as Jeremiel and Azrael)
Urian	Urjan, Uryan, Uriel
Uriel	Urian, Urjan, Uryan
Urjan	Urian, Uryan, Uriel
Uryan	Urjan, Urian, Uriel
Zachiel	Zadkiel; Satqiel; Tzadkiel; Zadakiel; Zidekiel; Tzadiqel; Tsadkiel
Zadakiel	Zadkiel; Satqiel; Tzadkiel; Zidekiel
Zadakiel	Zadkiel; Satqiel; Tzadkiel; Zidekiel; Tzadiqel; Tsadkiel; Zachiel

NAME	ALSO KNOWN AS
Zadkiel	Satqiel; Tzadkiel; Zadakiel; Zidekiel
Zadkiel	Satqiel; Tzadkiel; Zadakiel; Zidekiel; Tzadiqel; Tsadkiel; Zachiel
Zerachiel	Sariel; Sarakiel; Saraguel; Saraqael; Saraqel; Sahaqiel
Zidekiel	Zadkiel; Satqiel; Tzadkiel; Zadakiel
Zidekiel	Zadkiel; Satqiel; Tzadkiel; Zadakiel; Tzadiqel; Tsadkiel; Zachiel
Zophiel	Jophiel; Iofiel; Iophiel; Jofiel

ARCHANGEL IN CHARGE

If you are looking for a more detailed list of archangel roles then this may be useful for you. This list uses traditional roles as a guide but if you feel that a different angel will help your purpose more, then go with your own gut instinct. You will know – trust yourself.

This list just uses archangels. Some of the many thousands of angels hold similar roles.

TASK/SKILLS	HELPING ANGEL
Acting	Gabriel
Adoption	Gabriel
Alternative Healers	Raphael
Ambition	Michael
Arguments (Resolving)	Raguel
Armed Forces Personnel	Michael
Art	Gabriel
Artists	Jophiel
Awareness	Jophiel
Balance	Haniel
Beauty	Jophiel, Chamuel, Haniel, Gabriel
Birds	Ariel

Task/Skills	Helping Angel
Bouncers	Chamuel
Careers	Metatron, Chamuel
Charity	Metatron
Child Healing	Ariel
Childbirth	Gabriel
Children, Spirits	Sariel
Children's Spiritual Gifts	Metatron
Clairvoyance	Jeremiel
Comforting	Raphael
Company	Haniel
Compassion	Zadkiel, Jeremiel
Conception	Gabriel
Confidence	Zadkiel
Conflicts (Resolving)	Raguel
Contentment	Chamuel
Counsellors	Raphael
Courage	Michael
Creative Endeavours	Jophiel
Creative Insight	Uriel
Creativity	Gabriel, Uriel
Crossing Over	Azrael
Crystals	Haniel
Cures	Raphael
Dancing	Gabriel
Death	Azrael, Sariel
Decorating	Jophiel
Defending	Raguel
Design	Jophiel
Dieting	Metatron
Dignity	Haniel
Direction	Michael
Disasters	Uriel

Task/Skills	Helping Angel
Divine Guidance	Raziel
Divine Magic	Ariel
Doctors	Raphael
Dream Interpretation	Gabriel
Dreams	Ariel
Dying	Azrael
Earth Healing	Raphael, Uriel
Ecology	Uriel
Effort	Metatron
Empathy	Jeremiel
Empowering	Raguel
Enlightenment	Jophiel
Esoteric Materials	Raziel
Fairy Kingdoms	Ariel
Faith	Zadkiel
Fire	Uriel
Fish	Ariel
Fixing	Michael
Floods	Uriel
Flowers	Gabriel
Forgiveness	Zadkiel
Freedom	Metatron
Freedom Of Thought	Jophiel
Friends	Haniel
Gatekeeper	Chamuel
Gender Determination	Sandalphon
Gifted Children	Metatron
Good Causes	Metatron
Grace	Raphael
Gratitude	Chamuel
Grief Counselling	Azrael
Grieving	Azrael

TASK/SKILLS	HELPING ANGEL
Guidance	Zadkiel, Michael
Habits	Metatron
Happiness	Chamuel
Harmony	Raguel, Haniel
Healing	Ariel, Zadkiel, Metatron, Raphael, Sariel
Healing Animals	Ariel
Healing Knowledge	Uriel
Healing Remedies	Haniel
Health	Haniel, Raphael
Heavenly Armies	Gabriel
Hunters	Michael
Hygiene	Sariel
Ideas	Uriel
Individuality	Gabriel
Injustice	Michael
Inner Child	Gabriel
Inner Voice	Gabriel
Inspiration	Metatron
Inspiring	Gabriel
Intellectual Information	Uriel
Intelligence	Raziel
Intervention	Chamuel
Interviews	Haniel
Journalism	Gabriel
Joy	Chamuel, Raphael
Judge	Michael
Judgement Release	Zadkiel
Justice	Gabriel
Kabbalah	Sandalphon
Karma	Uriel
Kindness	Jeremiel
Knowledge	Raphael

Task/Skills	Helping Angel
Leadership	Michael
Liberation	Metatron
Libraries	Metatron
Life	Haniel
Life Changes	Jeremiel
Life Guidance	Raziel
Life Purpose	Chamuel
Light Work	Raphael
Light/Spiritual Workers	Michael
Lions	Ariel
Loneliness	Michael
Lost Items	Chamuel
Love	Gabriel, Raphael, Jeremiel
Magistrates	Michael
Manifestation	Raziel, Uriel
Memory	Zadkiel
Mending	Michael
Mercy	Michael, Jeremiel
Messenger	Gabriel
Midwives	Raphael, Sandalphon
Miracles	Gabriel, Michael, Raphael
Modelling	Gabriel
Moon	Gabriel
Moon Energy	Haniel
Moon Movement	Sariel
Motivating	Gabriel, Michael
Music	Gabriel, Sandalphon, Uriel
Mysteries	Gabriel
Natural Disasters	Uriel
Nature	Ariel
Nature Spirits	Ariel
Negativity	Michael

TASK/SKILLS	HELPING ANGEL
Nurses	Raphael
Open Mindedness	Jophiel
Organizations	Raguel
Passion	Haniel
Past Lives	Jeremiel
Patience	Michael
Peace	Chamuel
Peacemaking	Gabriel
Performing	Haniel
Persistence	Haniel
Police	Michael
Possessions	Chamuel
Spiritual Wisdom	Haniel
Students	Uriel
Studies	Uriel
Supportive	Michael
Teachers	Uriel
Teaching	Gabriel
Telecommunications	Gabriel
Television	Gabriel
Tenderness	Gabriel
Tests	Uriel
Therapists	Raphael
Third Eye	Raphael
Thunder	Uriel
Transformation	Uriel
Travellers/Travelling	Raphael
Truth	Gabriel, Michael
Unborn Babies	Sandalphon
Unconditional Love	Gabriel, Michael
Universal Mysteries	Raziel
Uplifting	Michael

TASK/SKILLS	HELPING ANGEL
Visions	Ariel, Gabriel
Visually Impaired	Raphael
Water	Ariel
Weather	Uriel
Wholeness	Raphael
Wild Animals	Ariel, Raphael
Witness	Metatron
World Events	Chamuel
World Peace	Chamuel
Writing	Gabriel, Uriel
Young Children	Gabriel

7

Fallen Angels

Fallen Angels

WHO WERE THE FALLEN ANGELS?

Satan is the most well known of the fallen angels and the leader of the fallen ones (later identified by some as Lucifer). Although I don't like to dwell on the so-called 'fallen angels', they do appear in various texts and I feel they should not be left out completely if I am to share with you a complete view!

Revelation 12:4 says, '*And his tail drew the third part of the stars of heaven and did cast them to earth.*' Satan was said to have deceived the whole world and was cast out, his angels with him: '*The great dragon was hurled down ... called the devil or Satan, who leads the whole world astray. He was hurled to the earth and his angels with him*' (Revelation 12:9).

Yet to call them 'Angels' goes against everything which is good, so many people still refuse to accept that there were (or are) fallen angels, recognizing them instead as negative energy or that which is without light. Some say that the name Satan does not refer to a specific 'angel' but is just representative of something negative, and that if you do not recognize this energy it does not exist. I think the debate will go on…

Many of these fallen angels once belonged to the choirs of angels and include such names as:

'FALLEN' ANGEL	MEANINGS OF NAME
Antichrist	Great Enemy of Humanity
Asmodeus	Demon of Lust and Anger
Azazel	The Standard Bearer of Hell
Balan	King of Hell
Beelzebub	Prince of Hell
Dagon	Phoenician Demon
Devil	The Evil One
Incubus	Woman Seducer
Leviathan	Sea Demon
Lucifer	The Fallen Light Bearer
Satan	The Greatest Fallen One
Succubus	Man Seducer
Zaebos	The Grand Count of Hell

AND HELL?

Many regard Hell as being a place of our own making – a place that exists only in our own minds. Another view of Hell is that it is the place in the other-side that we find ourselves if that is where we expect to end up, or feel we deserve to go. For those that follow and recognize the light, or the good, it is said that this place of Hell has no power.

Does the place of hell and damnation exist? Not for any normal souls, I wouldn't think!

HOW MANY FALLEN ANGELS WERE THERE?

The *Book of Enoch* says that there were 200 fallen angels (and it names around 20, if you include those names which have various spellings). Other sources suggest that as many as one third of all the angels became fallen angels. In 1460, Alphonso de Spina suggested that this number might reach 133,306,668!

WHY DID THE ANGELS FALL?

In some texts it is said that the angels fell because of man. Genesis 6:2 states that the angels *'saw the daughters of men … and took them as their wives'*, the start of the end for these angels!

St Augustine suggests the fall was due to pride and will. *'Good and bad angels have arisen … from a difference in their wills and desires.'*

OTHER REFERENCES TO 'BAD' ANGELS

John Milton and Dante

The stories of 'fallen angels' were further introduced through the literary works of the writers John Milton, and Dante. Dante was a great writer and poet who lived at the end of the Middle Ages, and is famous in particular for his work *The Divine Comedy*, in which the author travels down through Hell and Purgatory, before reaching Heaven. John Milton's *Paradise Lost* is his best-known work, and the work in which he writes most fully about the angels, including the fallen 'Lucifer'.

Daemons

According to Greek mythology, the word 'daemon' or 'daimon' was used to describe pretty well any spiritual being, as the literal translation is 'divine being'. The word was used for either bad or good spirits. The word was often used to describe angels, and an evil angel was also called a 'kakodaimon'.

8

Angels in
Culture

Angels in Culture

ANGELS IN ART

Artists have always painted angels. It is hard to know how much these earliest images dictate our expectations of what an angel might look like. Do angels really have halos and wings or do they choose to show themselves in that way because it is what we expect and what we feel comfortable with?

In traditional art, those depicted most often are Gabriel, Michael, Metatron, Raphael and Uriel. Michael makes a worthy subject for a portrait and is usually shown with his 'flaming sword', ready for battle. Michael is an obvious inspiration for religious art, being a protector of humankind.

Gabriel is the archangel most likely to be shown as a female angel. Modern artwork regularly shows angels as beautiful human women with wings, presenting a change in the perceived energy of angels from masculine to feminine.

Azrael is shown as the angel of death. He was greatly feared as the angel who stole away human souls. Now we recognize this role as one of comfort and friendship – an angel who helps souls over to the other-side, rather than snatching them away. Ancient artwork will reflect this traditional vision of a frightening figure of loss.

Although similar traits (like Michael being depicted with a sword) do flow through the different painters' ideas of what particular angels might look like, vast differences are also shown. Fra Angelico (c.1387–1455) painted the Angel Gabriel as part of a fresco called *The Annunciation*. Gabriel is dressed in a gown of reddish-bronze with his feet hidden (almost as if he could be floating). His hair is blonde and curly with a classical 'halo' of light around his head. He has a pair of large golden wings.

François Boucher (1703–70) painted *Angels and Doves* as an 'oil on canvas'. Boucher (the celebrated Rococo artist) draped his chubby-baby angels (or cherubs) in soft pink cloth and gave them the tiniest of bird-type wings.

In another, completely different style, William Blake (1757–1827) in his *Christ in the Sepulchre, Guarded by Angels*, a pair of creamy-white angels pray over the body of Christ. Their long white gowns drape over a human-like body. Each angel has high-pointing wings and the top half of the angels is surrounded by a soft golden glow.

ANGELS AND CELEBRITIES

People don't have the same fear of embarrassment talking about angels that they once had. Even people in the public eye are happy to talk about their own angels. Following an event to help publicize a project called 'A Gathering of Angels' (to support work which promotes the protection of children suffering from violence), author Pat Montandon asked many well-known people to draw and write about their own angels.

The project produced a book entitled *Celebrities and their Angels*, and contributors included ex-USSR president Mikhail Gorbachev, chat-show hosts Jay Leno and Oprah Winfrey and film stars including Burt Reynolds and Whoopi Goldberg. There are even entries by Archbishop Desmond Tutu and the Dalai Lama! Believing in angels, and admitting to the fact, is now an OK thing to do!

ANGELS IN FILMS AND TELEVISION SHOWS

Angels are portrayed in our modern television programmes and in films in much the way they were painted in Renaissance times. Modern interpretations of angels vary greatly. Here are some favourite classics.

Highway to Heaven

The angel 'Jonathan' was played by actor and director Michael Landon (star of the children's favourite *Little House on the Prairie*) in the hit TV series *Highway to Heaven*. Jonathan was the angel sent down by God, 'The Boss', to partner with ex-Californian policeman Mark Gordon. Their role was to help people see a better way of living and to act in the role of guardians, and it made for an entertaining and highly popular show.

The original movie *Highway to Heaven* was written by Landon, too, and he went on to write and direct many of the future episodes of the show. The show, which ran for many years on the American channel NBC, completed four seasons and finished halfway through a fifth after 108 episodes. The show featured many stars, including actor Dick Van Dyke.

Touched by an Angel

Another popular American television series, *Touched by an Angel* starred Roma Downey, who plays Monica, the soft-hearted angel dispatched to Earth to help people facing crossroads in their lives. Monica works under the watchful eye of her heavenly supervisor, Tess, played by actress Della Reese. The show has a massive fan base.

It's a Wonderful Life

James Stewart stars in this 1946 film classic. An angel shows the kindly but discouraged businessman what life would had been like if he had never existed, after George (played by Stewart) tries to take his own life by jumping off a snowy bridge. The film shares a kinship with Charles Dickens' *A Christmas Carol*, and is a timeless Christmas film favourite.

The Bishop's Wife

An angel named Dudley (Cary Grant) befriends an Episcopal bishop (David Niven) who is completely focused on raising money for his new church, and the bishop's wife (Loretta Young), who has become lonely and unhappy as her husband becomes lost in his work.Grant uses heavenly magic and charm to help the bishop raise the money and to rediscover the joy in life, and rekindle his relationship with his wife.

Wings of Desire

The sky over Berlin is full of angels wearing trench coats that listen to the tortured thoughts of humans below and try to comfort them. One of these souls, Damiel (Bruno Ganz), wishes to become mortal after falling in love with a beautiful trapeze artist, Marion (played by Solveig Dommartin). Peter Falk assists in the transformation by explaining the simple joys of human experience…like coffee and cigarettes!

This film is very much told from the angels' point of view and is shot in black and white. It only blossoms into colour when the angels see the realities of humankind. This highly acclaimed film won many awards and was later remade in 1998 into *City of Angels*, starring Nicolas Cage and Meg Ryan.

City of Angels

Angel Seth (Nicolas Cage) is an angel watching over Los Angeles. He begins to find his job difficult after he falls in love with Maggie, a beautiful heart surgeon, played by Meg Ryan. The attraction is mutual and soon his angelic state is a barrier rather than a gift. A choice must be made between his angelic duty and earthly love. This beautiful film was spoiled for me by its sad ending! Angel films should always have a happy ending … in my opinion!

Michael

A funny and sensitive Archangel Michael is played by actor John Travolta in this film directed by Nora Ephron. Michael – complete with large white wings – takes up residence at the Milkbottle Motel. After sorting out the financial problems of the lady owner he hangs around earth a little longer to smoke a few cigarettes, drink a few beers and enjoy a little dancing. When a couple of reporters discover the angel's whereabouts, the fun really begins…!

Charlie's Angels

The word 'angel' appears in many TV programme and film titles. In its broadest sense it offers a vision of someone who helps others. The classic *Charlie's Angels* (both the old series and the new films) are about three ex-police women, placed in a position of helping others. The ladies are not actual angels but, as the title suggests, they act as guardians to the helpless, working under the direction of the ever-invisible boss 'Charlie'.

Angel

Another, very unusual interpretation is *Angel*. *Angel* made its debut in 1999. The title character, played by David Boreanaz, is a vampire tormented by the possession of a human soul. The show developed from the same character he played in *Buffy The Vampire Slayer* – Buffy's love interest for three seasons.

Angel was born as 'Liam' in Ireland 1727. He later adopted the name Angelus, meaning 'the one with the angelic face' or 'the dark side of God', which becomes the fallen or negative side of the character. The Angel – 'vampire with a soul' half of the character, works with his group of friends and colleagues to rid the world of evil. A modern slant on the story, and a very popular series! Again, not a 'real' angel, nor does it pretend to be, but a character playing the part of an earthly guardian just the same.

ANGELS AND MUSIC

'The seventh angel sounded his trumpet and there were loud voices in heaven, which said: "The kingdom of the world has become the kingdom of our Lord and of his Christ, and he will reign for ever and ever."'

REVELATIONS 11.15

Do angels really play trumpets and harps in heaven? Angels certainly sing in pure bliss. Their voices sound like a thousand instruments of joy and love. Many people have heard the sound of the spheres and I am one of those. But I'm not alone!

The American writer Ralph Waldo Emerson once wrote *'All the great interrogatories, like questioning angels, float in on its waves of sound.'* It makes me wonder if he heard them too.

Lyn remembered a time when as a child she used to run and play in the tumble weeds in the California Central Valley. Lyn was afflicted with polio as a baby, and grew up playing in the fields with her brothers. They lived right out in the country and spent a lot of time alone. She would play in these fields for hours and the only thing that would make them stop and stand still was the beauty of the celestial music!

Often it would sound like angels in the sky, and she described it as being a little like the Mormon Tabernacle Choir! They heard the music all of the time, and she says it was quite wonderful. As a small child Lyn felt that she seemed to know of a higher being, and was left in no doubt there was a God because she felt his existence.

9

Angels in Religion

Angels in Religion

Angels are not tied to any religious groups. They belong to people of all religious beliefs and those with no beliefs at all. The Hebrews see angels as 'beings of love and grace' and the Jews recorded vast texts in the Old Testament about how the angels helped them in their battle for freedom. The Archangel Gabriel dictated the Koran to Mohammed.

DIFFERENT RELIGIONS, DIFFERENT INTERPRETATIONS

Angel names and roles vary from religion to religion, although nearly all traditions show 'angel-like' beings or 'beings of light', even if they do not actually call them angels. Most religions see angels as messengers and servants of God, and beings that work in His name.

Some religions represent angels as protectors but others, such as the Judeo-Christian tradition, see angels more as spiritual beings that help you work through your problems, rather than taking the problems away – following the idea of humans being born with 'free will' and being sent to earth to learn lessons. In the Garden of Gethsemane, angels appeared to Jesus to give him the strength he needed to endure his death, rather than to save him from death.

Martin Luther King Jr – Working with Faith

A modern interpretation of this would be the story of Martin Luther King Jr, who as a 26-year-old minister with a young wife and baby was called upon to lead the campaign against black segregation in the American South. He was a strong believer in Jesus and his religious teachings, and called for spiritual assistance when he was faced with the full force of personal hatred the Civil Rights movement provoked.

As he prayed 'I just can't face it alone!' King felt a presence with him, and although the presence did not 'save him' from his role completely, it did make him realize he was not alone, which made his hardships easier to bear. He felt that he was being assisted by higher beings. Just days later a bomb blasted his house; luckily no one was hurt. Rather than 'pulling him down' the incident gave him renewed strength, as he warned his followers not to follow violence with violence.

'If it wasn't for that black pastor, there'd be many a man dead tonight!' a police officer was heard to have said later.

JEWISH TRADITION

Angels are also very prominent in the Jewish religion. Jewish teaching about angels goes back to the scriptures: the Torah (the first five books of the Bible), the Prophets and the Writings. Genesis chapter 3 mentions the Cherubim guarding the gates of Eden (with their flaming swords) after Adam and Eve are banished. Abraham receives a visit from an angel to tell him that he and Sarah will have a child (Genesis 18), and in another incident, an angel appears to Moses out of the burning bush (Exodus 3:2).

This is just a few of the many excerpts that show angels working on many levels with humans.

Mal'ach is the Hebrew word for 'angel'. Many believe that the role of the angels is to distance God from man so that God remains invisible and somewhat intangible to us. Angels appear as a sort of high-level 'entourage' to God. In Isaiah 6, the angels are to the left and right of God, as he is seated on his heavenly throne. Jewish literature does show angels as having individual personalities, which many other religions might interpret as different attributes and roles rather than 'personality' as such.

The ancient Jews wrote the apocryphal literature which featured angels. The work deals with the end of days and is filled with the doings of angels. The literature mentions angels such as Shalgiel (the angel of snow), Ram'amiel (the angel of thunder) and Ra'asiel (angel of earthquakes). Angels are said to have disagreed with God about creating human beings at all. The angels suggested that people would sin against God!

Part of the rabbinical teaching includes two angels who follow people home on Shabbat (the Sabbath) to check that the home is ready. One of these angels is good and one is bad. The angels check that the challah wine is prepared and that the candles are lit, ready for Shabbat.

ANGELS IN THE NEW TESTAMENT

Angels are prominent in the New Testament, and are mentioned around 165 times! They sometimes take on the appearance of humans to carry out God's tasks as they often frightened humans with their own appearance. As the shepherds were visited by the angels to proclaim the birth of Jesus, the heavenly host announced 'do not be afraid': I imagine they made quite a sight!

Angels were made by God, '…things invisible, thrones, powers, rulers and authorities…' (Colosians 1:16), and they were created before humans. Usually they are unseen but appear in a bodily form only when they have no other choice. The Bible quotes many angels appearing as messengers of God, most famously the archangel Gabriel making the announcement to Mary in Nazareth that she was to give birth to a son and that she was to call him Jesus.

Jesus regularly communicated with angels. He taught that they did not marry and were genderless, and also that they were created by God directly. Jesus taught that angels watch over little children (Matthew 18:10) and guard humankind on earth. He said that at his second coming, the angels would return with him (Matthew 25:31). Angels appeared on a regular basis to the Apostles after the crucifixion of Jesus to help them to keep their faith and to protect them from their enemies.

Angels are shown performing many other roles too, including ministering, encouraging and comforting. An angel appeared to Paul to comfort him during a shipwreck (Acts 27:23) and help give him the strength he needed to come through the hardship.

The New Testament warns against worshipping angels, tempting though it might be. The Book of Hebrews suggests that only Jesus was to be worshipped and that the angels follow Jesus. Even the angels agreed. In Revelation 22:8-9 an angel scolds John for falling down in worship. The angel reminds him '…I am a fellow-servant with you … worship God.'

ANGELS OF THE KABBALAH

'Kabbalah' (the Jewish mystical tradition) translates from the Hebrew word meaning 'to receive'. Angels are shown to guide humans and help them on their earthly path. One teaching says that an angel walks in front of every human saying the words, 'make way for the image of the blessed holy one'.

Two thoughts of Kabbalistic mysticism developed, 'the work of creation' (ma'aseh bereishit) and 'the work of the chariot' (ma'aseh merkabah). One works with the creation or design of the cosmos and the other with how humans should work and approach God. The mystics enlarged on the more ancient traditions of angelic messengers and guides and developed new traditions including many chants and principles relating to angel names. Much of this was sacred information, kept secret, and made difficult to understand.

Archangel Metatron is highlighted in the Jewish 'Hekhalot' literature as the leader of the people of Israel. Other angels are popular, including Michael, Gabriel, Raphael and Uriel. Each could be called upon as part of a bedtime prayer routine (although not everyone agreed with the praising of angels, feeling that no link to God was required and working with angels in this way would distract from the Creator himself). Belial (or Samiel) was recognized as an evil angel (rather like Satan or Lucifer).

Kabbalists also developed the idea of the Ten Sefirot (Divine Energies). An angel might be directly associated with these (Gabriel with Yesod for example). The belief developed that humans were not as spiritual as angels, but that angels do not have 'free will', working only under the direction of God, and each with a specific role or skill.

ARCHANGEL	ASSOCIATED SEFIRAH (of the Divine Energies)
Metatron	Keter (Crown)
Raziel	Chochmah (Wisdom)
Cassiel	Binah (Understanding)
Zadkiel	Chesed (Kindness)
Samael	Gevurah (Justice)
Michael	Tiferet (Splendour)
Anael	Netzach (Victory)
Raphael	Hod (Glory)
Gabriel	Yesod (Foundation)
Sandalphon	Malchut (Kingdom)

Each person was believed to have a spiritual guardian. Teachings say that angels are created by God, but that it is possible for humans to ascend and become angels (through good works).

BASIC BELIEFS RELATING TO ANGELS IN DIFFERENT RELIGIONS

RELIGION	ANGELS	TYPE OF CELESTIAL BEINGS
Buddhism	'Dharmapalas' and 'dharma' are seen as beings of protection.	'Devas' or celestial beings. In Tibetan Buddhism, 'bodhisattvas' are considered to be enlightened spirits who show themselves as light emanations. These devas are not normally seen to interfere in human lives.
Christianity – Catholicism	Archangel Gabriel, Archangel Michael and the Archangel Raphael.	Seen as a direct link with God and the messengers and servants of the divine. The Catholic angelology was pulled together by St Thomas Aquinas who developed the hierarchy (or 'choirs of angels') which we still use today. Catholicism teaches that the angels speak to the inner person. Catholics can ask for angelic help in the form of prayer.
Christianity – Orthodox	The most important are Archangels Michael, Gabriel, Raphael, Uriel, Selaphiel, Jehudiel, Barachiel and Jeremiel. Satan is recognized as a fallen angel.	Workers and messengers of God. Angels and archangels seen as part of the hierarchy of 9 powers in Orthodox tradition. Pictured in a physical way as looking like man or having 6 wings (but not having physical bodies).

RELIGION	ANGELS	TYPE OF CELESTIAL BEINGS
Christianity – Protestant	Biblical angels are prominent. Good and bad angels are recognized.	Many Protestant theologians discourage praying to angels and do not follow the angelic hierarchy (seeing it as a pagan tradition). 'Angels' are recognized as genderless and invisible beings.
Hinduism	No individual angels but spirits who act in a similar way. The 'divas' (or 'shining ones') who work on the higher planes, and 'asuras' (evil spirits). 'Lipika' regulates karma and 'angiris' who looks over sacrifices.	Beings are sometimes pictured in physical form.
Islam	Archangel Jabra'il (Gabriel and other variant spellings,) who revealed the Koran to Mohammad. Also Mika'il (Michael), Izrafil, Izra'il, Munkar and Nakir. Shaitan ('the evil one'), a member of the 'jinn' rather than an actual angel.	Messengers from Allah to the world. Angels shown as having specific roles. Beliefs include each person having their own guardian angels. Angels are said to keep records of lives both good and bad.

RELIGION	ANGELS	TYPE OF CELESTIAL BEINGS
Judaism	Archangel Michael is a guardian of the people of Israel. Also important are Uriel, Gabriel and Raphael.	Seen as messengers and guardians again, and also carrying out the work of God. Spiritual beings with no bodily form – although where they are seen as having physical form, Maimonides the Jewish sage wrote that the descriptions of physical angels were metaphorical. Angels are not worshiped as it is believed that only God decides the fate of humans.
Mormonism	Founder of Mormonism Joseph Smith was visited by the angel Moroni.	Mormons see angels as beings who have lived on the earth previously (which other religions and beliefs would call spirits), beings who have previously incarnated – lived as humans. Angels are seen as ministering spirit or messengers as with other religions. Angels are also seen to comfort, warn and protect.

10

Angels in Our Lives

Angels in Our Lives

ANGELS IN MY LIFE

A belief in angels is something that has always been with me. I remember an incident from my early childhood which became buried in my psyche. It did not surface again until many years later.

Sensing Angels

My parents, my sisters and I were staying on the Isle of Wight (off the South Coast of England). The island is famous for its beaches. The sand was like white powder I remember, beautiful and perfect for an English beach holiday. My first angel experience happened while on this family holiday.

My mum had packed a large picnic and was busy laying things out ready for our lunch while my sisters and I made sandcastles with our buckets and spades. No castle is complete without a moat, so after the castle had been built, my sister Debbie and I started the journey backwards and forwards to the sea to collect water in our buckets. When you're five

years old you don't realize that the water sinks straight back into the sand! That moat was never going to be full, but we had lots of fun trying. The tide was going out as we made each trip across the hot sand, backwards and forwards, with every journey getting longer and longer.

It was nearly lunch time but the moat was no fuller! 'Perhaps just one more trip across the boiling hot sand before a sandwich and a plastic beaker full of warm orange squash?' The sea was now a long walk away. At the last moment I'd decided to take my rubber float with me. Perhaps I'd have a little dip in the water before the long walk back up the beach? I remember reaching the water's edge and stepping in for a little paddle. The water was cool and soothing on my feet, burnt from the hot sand. Perhaps I'd wade in a little further?

In seconds I was bobbing up and down in the sea. My family were way off into the distance, and the beach was now crowded with families and children, but in no time at all I could feel myself being swept out to sea! The light breeze had picked up and I was being pulled towards a nearby crop of rocks. I didn't understand a lot about death but I knew at that moment I was going to drown and there was nothing I could do about it. Panic started to rise within me – 'should I shout for help?' No one was even close by. Would my family notice I was missing? Would they come and save me? I realized they wouldn't.

It was then that I understood that I was not alone. I felt surrounded by a peaceful presence, which seemed to communicate with me somewhere inside my head ... a voice that was not a voice. 'What was it?' I was enveloped by a serene calm, and an inner contact that I realized was separate from my own consciousness – it was something that wasn't me. The voice spoke to me inside my mind.

'You can drown if you want to ... or you can swim to shore,' the presence seemed to say.

'Swim to shore? But I can't swim?'

'The presence will help you, you can swim to shore.'

I felt in control. OK, I can do this, and I started to move my arms as I had before but this time I felt stronger. I was moving forwards, I was beating the waves. Closer and closer I got to the shore, stronger and stronger I felt, and all the time being moved forward by an unseen force and guardian. Something or someone that wanted to help me...

Suddenly I was there and I stepped onto the beach. But it wasn't so suddenly really. I was a long way out and it had taken a while. Children and adults were paddling on the edge of the water. Everything seemed normal and the presence had gone. I bent down to pick up my rubber float and I noticed that the air had come out. My float hadn't helped me to stay afloat at all, but I knew I couldn't swim, or could I? Had I suddenly learnt to swim?

Excited now, I jumped back into the waves – 'I can swim!' I yelled and promptly sank underneath the waves. I hadn't learnt to swim at all. Confusion racked my young brain and I realized that something unusual had happened. An inner voice, a presence, had saved me from drowning.

I ran back up the beach with a mixture of relief and panic: relief that I was alive but panic that I now had to find my parents. My family was even further away than I'd imagined, but as I rushed breathlessly to the group, my mother looked a little concerned.

'Where have you been?' she asked me.

'I nearly drowned!' I cried.

'Never mind, have a sandwich...!'

And that was the end of that! It wasn't mentioned again and I forgot about it until many years later. I didn't call it an angel then, but now I wonder if it was?

Hearing Angels

Many years later and with two daughters of my own, I had another experience. In October 1997, flicking through TV channels, I caught the tail end of Granada TV's magazine chat show *This Morning* with Richard Madeley and Judy Finnigan. The show had an unusual guest this particular day – Angel writer Diana Cooper. I was spellbound by Diana's accounts of angel experiences in people's lives. Here were *normal* people having what appeared to be *paranormal* experiences. Totally fascinated by the real possibility of the existence of angels, I went out and bought her angel book, *A Little Light on Angel*s, the following day.

A million thoughts went through my head! Was this possible? Were there really angels? And, rather bizarrely – what a cool job – I'd like to do that! Ironically, in less than six years I was sitting on the set of *This Morning* and this time I was the angel expert ... but I digress!

It was shortly afterwards that I had one of the most extraordinary experiences of my whole life – and for no obvious or apparent reason other than I'd wished it so! My youngest daughter Georgina was suffering from a sickness bug, and I was afflicted with exhausted Mum syndrome. Looking after children is a tiring job – looking after a sick child is worse.

I soon ran out of clean sheets and was rapidly running out of blankets and towels – sick children make a lot of mess! I made a 'management decision' and decided to make her up a bed on the bathroom floor. In my exhausted state, I somehow imagined that by being nearer to the toilet it would save me from any more washing – it didn't.

I crept back to bed for the fifth or sixth time and was just drifting back to sleep when I heard her call me again, 'Mum!' The lack of sleep was beginning to take its toll. I dragged myself back into the bathroom where my poor sweating daughter lay in total exhaustion – it was then that I remembered the angel book. I muttered, half under my breath and half aloud, '…where are the angels when you want one – YOU look after her because I am too tired – I just can't do this any more!'

Rather oddly and right on cue I suddenly became aware of an 'orchestral-type' music filling the bathroom! Looking round in confusion I assumed that some type of event or celebration must have started in the fields at the back of our house. Wondering who might possibly be up at this hour (and playing musical instruments in the middle of the night), I decided to investigate.

Stepping into the bath so that I could open and look out of the bathroom window, I peered into the moonlit fields! I realized rather quickly that the music was not coming from outside at all … so where was it coming from? I carefully climbed out of the bath, stepping over my daughter, who was now sleeping soundly!

I briefly considered other ideas. 'Had my husband decided to get out of bed and turn on the TV?' I popped my head outside the door and listened for a moment before realizing that the music was definitely coming from inside the bathroom – there was now no doubt! Something clicked in my brain at that very moment … were angels replying to my call for help? I guessed they were!

My sense of reality had been 'shot to ribbons'. I had to conclude that the music in the bathroom was being played by some unseen spiritual beings. I know I was tired but I was not imagining this – it was real. I'd asked angels to come and help me and they'd arrived in grand style. My daughter slept through the whole thing and awoke sickness-free the following morning! Coincidence? Maybe, maybe not!

The experience opened up more questions than it had given me answers, and made me reflect on experiences I'd had in the past – experiences that also seemed to fit into the 'unknown', or perhaps 'unexplained' category!

Seeing Angels

Not many people are lucky enough to see angels. They are seen by the dying or those having near-death experiences, by people having miraculous healings, and people going through deep crises in their lives. Sometimes they are seen for no apparent reason at all – but at the time of writing this book, I haven't seen an angel myself (as far as I know!).

When I was a young girl, my father used to be a keen fisherman. His fishing friend Bert and his wife Rachael (Aunty Pip) would often come to visit. They would bring their tent when we went caravanning, and I remember them buying little battery-operated lamps for each of us children so we could read late into the night while we lay in our caravan bunk beds. 'Uncle Bert' and 'Aunty Pip' were a big part of my childhood.

Each year the fishermen held a ball. A meal was followed by speeches and presentations of the winning cups for the best fisherman in each class. Dancing followed in the traditional ballroom style and my sisters and I often went along. We went to other dances, too, and one year Pip made my sisters and I long skirts to wear at them – everyone wore long dresses to formal occasions then!

One holiday I posed for the camera. I was about 12 years old and had a big floppy hat on and dark sunglasses. 'You look like Miss World,' she said. 'One day you're going to be famous!'

Many years passed and we lost contact with them, but when it was my parents' Golden Wedding anniversary we searched out their old friends Bert and Pip to join us for a surprise party. The party was a great success and so began a renewed friendship with the couple. It was strange to develop a friendship with them as the adult I now was!

Regularly they would call at my parents' house for meals and I always made a point of calling in for a chat when they were around. Sadly, Bert became ill with cancer, and when he died a short while later Pip's life fell apart. With no children, Bert was everything to Pip and Pip was everything to Bert. So one day, when I felt Bert come to me with a message from the 'other-side', I felt I had to call Pip and tell her what I had experienced. It was a difficult decision to make. What if she thought I was mad? What if I made things worse? Eventually I decided to just make the call.

I almost backed out as I picked up the phone but I took a deep breath and told her I'd felt Bert come through to me. She didn't doubt my word for one minute, but the clincher for her was when I explained that the spirit of Bert had said she was having problems with her television. 'Yes,' she said, 'I have the television man calling round to fix it today.'

I understood later that the telephone call was a turning point for her and she did make some small improvement with her deep grief. Unhappily, Pip was ill herself and within a few weeks had to have hospital treatment. The condition was worse than we had realized and the operation to remove a tumour on her neck would mean that she would need several weeks of convalescence to recover. With no other close family or friends in a position to take on this difficult task, my mum readily agreed that Pip should come and stay for two weeks.

She looked exhausted when she arrived from the hospital. The scar was very large and she looked very small and frail. She was also very weak and it was obvious that it was going to be a long two weeks! I started calling round a couple of times a day to see if I could do anything to help. Things went from bad to worse, as my father slipped and fell and ended up in hospital with a broken arm! Now mum had two invalids to look after, so I made more regular trips round to help out. By the second week, I was able to take mum out for a couple of hours to pick up some shopping. Dad and Pip were managing to cooperate and do simple things like make a pot of tea – each with their own 'best side!' One would open the fridge and one would lift out the milk carton!

At the end of the second week, Pip went home. With the help of family and friends and a lovely neighbour, she managed to make a recovery.

But it was only a temporary thing; a couple of months later she had to go back into hospital again. This time even she knew how serious it was, and when she came back to the house to convalesce again, mum and I both knew she wasn't going to make it this time.

This second visit was much harder for her and she was too weak to get out of bed except to use the toilet. I now called in several times a day. I would pop into her room for maybe only two minutes at a time – it was as much as she could manage.

Near the end of the week she managed to sit in the armchair, and she asked me if I would do some healing on her. As I held my hands over her frail body, I once again felt the presence of her dead husband come to me and I was able to give her the message that he was with us. A large tear dropped down her cheeks and she told me she was ready to go with him.

'He's bringing you some flowers,' I said. 'Freesias.'

'Yes,' she confirmed, 'they are very special to us. We had them at our wedding and Bert had a freesia as his "buttonhole" on his wedding suit.'

I am a medium, but I still felt like such a beginner. I have only realized that some of the strange paranormal experiences that I'd had all of my life were contacts from 'the other-side', and I still felt awkward and uncomfortable when passing on a 'message'.

As I continued the healing, she started to ask me more questions about my work. What happens when we cross over to the other-side? Are our loved ones there to meet us? I told her about everything I'd learnt and she smiled. We joked about me getting famous and she reminded me about how she'd called me 'Miss World' when I was a child. She loved that fact that I'd been on TV the week she'd been in hospital. She loved telling the nurses that I was 'her niece'.

She started to look tired so I finished the healing. Don't worry, I teased, I'll fly over when you are asleep and continue the healing then. 'I'll bring over a few angels to help me,' I laughed. I'd had many 'out-of-body experiences' in the past where I'd remained aware and conscious of my experiences at the time.

I was teasing her about the angels wasn't I? I certainly didn't realize I had the power to 'summon' angels, but she certainly put me right the following day.

'Those flaming angels came and woke me up in the night!' she said crossly. But she laughed. She was serious!

'I woke up to all this racket, and the room was full of them. I could see you in the room too,' she said. ' You were sitting on the chair in the corner!' And a tear ran down her face.

Well I'd like to say that I remember this out-of-body flight, but I don't! It didn't seem to matter one bit. Pip had seen – and heard – the angels, in all their glory. Something changed after that. We all knew the end was near but she wasn't in the least bit worried. She knew without a shadow of a doubt that 'her Bert' and the angels would be there to meet her.

She died, less than a week later, but she left me with the most wonderful gift. Through her eyes, I'd 'seen' angels. With one foot in this world, and one foot in the next she'd been able to see what most of us are unable to see ... a 'choir of angels'.

Several months later she came back to see me in a dream. Even with all the experiences I've had, I still sometimes doubt that it's real. But it was real. She appeared to me in a way in which I'd never known her – as a younger woman with jet-black hair. My mum told me later that she had looked the way I described her. She just popped back to say goodbye. It was her.

Thank you Pip, it was a pleasure to look after you. God bless you in your new home. I know you're happy. And thank you for a gift that will stay with me my whole life.

THE BELIEF IN ANGELS

The appearance of angels in visitations to humans actually has a name of its own – 'Angelophany'. Most angel visitations, however, are more thoughts and feelings rather than a full-blown visitation, which is rare and usually related to major events, like the angel Gabriel appearing to Mary, or during times of great crisis.

What Do Angels Look Like?

People describe angels in many different ways. Some see tall beings, '…taller than the room. His head went through the ceiling and his feet, if there were any, disappeared through the floor.'

Some people see beings of light. 'I knew it was an angel. The light was so bright and clear. The light filled the whole room. You would expect to be blinded because the light was so strong but I could see it was clearly an angel.'

> *'…and saw two angels in white, seated where Jesus' body had been, one at the head and the other at the foot.'*
>
> JOHN 20:12

Julia and her twin sister Amanda were very close and shared everything, so Julia believed her sister when she told her about her own angel encounter. One night, not long after their mother died, Amanda was asleep in bed when something woke her up. On her table beside the bed was a photograph of their parents, and hovering over the picture was what she described as a 'golden cherub-type figure'. It was about eight inches in length. It radiated and shimmered in a golden colour. It was about four feet away from her head.

She wasn't frightened by it, she just watched. Finding it hard to believe what she had seen, she turned away for a few moments before turning back again, but it was still there, hovering. She turned away three times and each time she turned back it was still there. It stayed for around a minute.

Both Julia and Amanda believe that the little angel was showing them that their parents were safely with the angels on 'the other-side'.

Variety is the spice of life and Angels are no different. Another person described their angel descending at great speed, and that the angel was 'naked and hairless'. On another occasion this same angel was dressed in a white gown with a thin line of gold piping. He had shoulder-length brown hair, which was slightly curly.

Nick wrote and told me about the night his own angel appeared to him. He told me the angel was standing in his bedroom and he saw her in the corner of his eye. She looked beautiful and she just smiled. Her wings were especially pretty because they were see-through but very colourful. She was the most beautiful thing he had ever seen.

Angels in the Guise of Men and Women

There are many recorded instances of mysterious strangers appearing at the most useful of times. The car breaks down on a country lane and with no phone or house in sight; a stranger comes strolling along with just the right equipment in their backpack to fix the car. This stranger gives a cheery wave and when you turn around to offer them a small thank you, they seem to have disappeared into the night! Can angels appear in human form?

*'Be not forgetful to entertain strangers,
for thereby some have entertained angels unawares.'*

HEBREWS 13:2

Barbara wrote from the United States to tell me she was twenty-four weeks pregnant in 1998, with a seven-month-old baby at home, when she was in a tragic car accident. She remembers very little about the rescue and being flown by helicopter to the hospital.

When she was home recovering, several people at the accident scene, including her sister, told her two men in a coal truck stopped to check the scene of the accident. They said they were Emergency Medical Technicians, but later police were not able to locate them by the names they supplied. Even the place the strangers said that they worked at did not exist.

Barbara and her sister are certain they were angels in disguise. She needed to live for her two babies, she says, and they are all happy and healthy today.

June emailed me her experience. Was it an angel? It certainly sounds like one to me.

June and her family had been away on a visit to Scotland and when they got back home they found that the catch on the door had slipped, which meant they were unable to get into the house. They tried and tried to break into their back door but it would not move. June decided that the best course of action would be to go to a quiet place in the garden and just pray for help to come. What had she got to lose?

She told me that in less than five minutes, a complete stranger walked up to them and asked if they were in trouble and could he help! June did say that she had thought it might be her neighbour's father, as this man had appeared 'as if from nowhere at all' and in his shirtsleeves! With little difficulty he managed to break the small window in the front door and lift up the catch. They were in! June turned and gave the helpful stranger a kiss on the cheek. She even asked him if she could get him something as a thank you, but the gentleman refused any compensation.

June went round to her neighbour's the following day to say thank you, but it wasn't the neighbour's father after all. June did try and find out the identity of the stranger but no one knew who he was. She told me that she had not seen him before and had never seen him since. She always wondered if the man was her guardian angel.

This gentleman came to reassure Dodie and give her a little glimpse into her future. She certainly found it comforting. Some of the more dramatic stories occur when we 'hand over our problems' for God to deal with in his own way.

Where did this stranger come from and how did he know so much about her and her family? I'll let Dodie tell the story herself:

'In June of 2000 things were really going wrong. I was dealing with Irritable Bowel Syndrome and working for a dentist who was causing me undue stress. We had just applied for a home loan, and we were hoping to get a new house and move out into the country.

Our daughter was living away from home and she was also miserable. Our 14-year-old son was being a typical boy. My husband was a truck driver and was away two to three nights a week. Something needed to happen and fast. I kept telling my mother that if we didn't get the house, it wasn't meant to be and that God had other plans for us.

At 3.30 on that Tuesday, the lady from the bank called and said we were approved but, not for that house. I was a little disheartened, so I went to the Lord in prayer and I said, "Lord, I can't take much more so I'm laying all my problems in your lap."

The very next day at work we had a new patient admitted, whom I had never met or seen before. As we were walking to the treatment room, this man, Greg was his name, touched my stomach and said, "We need to pray…" As I was getting him seated he said, "You were a little upset about not getting the house yesterday…"

Well, he had my attention. How did he know this? He said that God had a bigger and better house in mind. He also told me that I needed to quit going home every day and locking myself in my room. Only God would have known this, but, I was so stressed out from the job and the boss that I was doing this. Next he gave me some information about my son. He then told me that our son was on a fence post, he could fall either way, being bad or good. How did he know I had kids? He told me that my husband was being faithful and would soon be home more often; he even said that God said we would be together forever! How did he know I had doubts?

At the time of writing this [2001], we have a bigger house in a new town. My husband has a new trucking job, and he's only working one night a week. He makes enough money to enable me to stay home, and now my job is taking care of him and my son.

And my illness? For the last year I weighed between 83 and 86 lbs *[about 6 stones]. I was referred to a new doctor who found that I was suffering from hyper-acidity. He put me on a new medicine, and now I weigh about 125 lbs [8¾ stones].*

I thank God every day for my guardian angel named Greg who is about six feet tall! I now know angels come in all sizes. Praise God!'

Maybe this is a lesson to us all? Trust in your God to provide the perfect outcome. We are not always aware of the bigger picture. We are not usually aware of what is coming next in the big plan.

Angels in Dreams

'He had a dream in which he saw a stairway resting on the earth, with its top reaching to heaven, and the angels of God were ascending and descending on it.'

GENESIS 28:12

Seeing a full-blown manifestation can be a frightening experience and angels do take the opportunity to show themselves to us in other ways. When the mind is in 'dream-state', it is better able to cope with a visitation experience. Many people have seen angels in this way.

Adam had been studying a book on spirituality and began exploring how this might interact with his own life, and if in fact a spirit life really existed or not. He explained how he found the book very hard going, as it was rather intellectual.

Determined to read the book anyway he decided the best course of action would be to read a little bit every night before going to sleep. After the very first night, however, Adam had a strange experience, which he believes may have been a result of studying the book. He described falling asleep and having what felt like a series of short 'dream-like' states. Each time, he believes, he was taken from his bed by angels. Sometimes he saw them and sometimes he just felt them. He believes he was taken to heaven.

He explained to me that he felt he had been to this place previously, and described it as a beautiful place, covered in clouds the colour of the sunset. Heaven houses masses and masses of angels, although it is not crowded, because Adam found it 'infinite'. It was wonderful to be taken to this holy place, as it is so peaceful and full of love. The trips, he explained seemed to happen one after another and no sooner was he back in bed than he was being shown another part of heaven. Not all of the experience felt like a dream and Adam felt that at least some of the time he was partly conscious whilst it was happening.

On the last occasion he believed he was honoured and privileged to see the great Archangel Michael, who Adam described as absolutely huge and very important. He held his sword in front of him with the point directed downwards, and he had his head bowed.

Angels Helping

If you look through some of the chapters in this book you will discover that there are angels for pretty well everything. There are angels who can help you unblock sinks, angels who can find you a trolley without a wonky wheel at the supermarket, and angels to help you prepare for a big speech. There are even angels who will help you to pick a car. Pick a car? Yes! That's right!

Vanessa has her own car angel. I'll let her explain:

'I am at a very transitional stage in my life. This is the time in life that we make some drastic changes. I had just finished school and was looking for a job; the only thing was that my parents live in cities that are not the ideal places for transportation. So borrowing the car from my Dad was becoming increasingly hard.

After a couple months of searching I landed a job with one of the leading wireless communication companies. Finally, I found myself in a position to purchase a used car. For the longest time, I thought about what car I wanted, but what could I afford? I was in some major financial debt after school and I did not have the credit history to finance a car loan.

Once again, my Dad had graciously offered to help me out. So we co-signed the loan together. However this whole time I was deliberating the decision about getting a car at this particular time because I was very irresponsible with money, and was trying to rectify my financial situation.

I have always had a fascination with angels and communicate with them whenever I can. I am habitually scared of everything and always call on St Michael [Archangel Michael] to protect me. I also knew of St Gabriel as a messenger from God [Archangel Gabriel]. So I prayed to Gabriel to send me some sort of message, if getting this car was such a great idea. A week had passed and still no signs had come. The dealership was hounding me to come and pick up the car and sign the papers, so after waiting the week I finally went to pick up my car.

At this point I was still very apprehensive about my decision, but there was nothing I could do now. So I brought the car home. A couple of days later my Mum asked to borrow my car for an errand and I gladly agreed without thinking anything of it. When my Mum arrived home later that day, she asked me about the sticker I had placed on my car. I told her I hadn't placed a sticker on it, but she insisted there was one and took me to see. There on the back of my car was a sticker, and when I saw it I almost fainted. In a very italic-looking print it said "GABRIEL"! From that moment on, all my fears subsided!'

Angels of Mons

In August 1914, a whole host of angels were said to have come to the aid of the British forces facing the Germans, in Mons, Belgium. Eyewitness accounts vary as to exactly what happened, but this story is special because there were multiple witnesses to the event!

British troops saw a ghostly army led by a white figure on horseback. Some people saw figures with wings, and others saw these glowing beings suspended in mid-air. Some soldiers later claimed to have seen Archangel Michael himself, and as the stories about the angelic army spread, more soldiers shared their own experiences of the ghostly helpers. Even German prisoners claimed to have seen the spiritual visitors. Curious indeed!

Recent studies suggest that the whole thing never happened at all. Either way, the story of angels protecting troops lifted the morale of the British forces and the story appears to have been encouraged at the time. Perhaps we'll never know if it ever happened or not.

11

Angels and Children

Angels and Children

Many believe there are special angels whose primary role is to protect children. In fact younger children in particular seem to have the ability to see angels, perhaps because they don't realize that others can't! They seem to have a special relationship with the heavenly realms. Is it because they have so recently arrived from heaven themselves?

Fairy Man

When my eldest daughter was just three years old I believe she saw an angel. It was the week my grandmother had died. She was in her nineties, so I was consoling myself that it was 'her time'. I had spent a lot of time with her in the weeks before she died, sitting by her bedside talking and sharing stories together. We had become very close.

My daughter was really too young to realize what 'died' meant, so she did not understand the significance of her off-hand comment a few days later. We were playing together, sitting on the living-room carpet, when she became totally distracted. Looking up at the ceiling, and very excited, she pointed at what she could see.

'Mummy look! There's a "fairy man!"'

Was it an angel sent to check that we were OK, or perhaps it was the spirit of my grandmother? Either way, it was fine with me and moments later we carried on playing as if nothing had happened! But it had!

> *'See that you do not look down on one of these little ones.*
> *For I tell you that their angels in heaven always see the*
> *face of my Father in heaven.'*
>
> MATTHEW 18:10

Here's another amazing story.

Baby sees Angels

When Theresa's daughter was fifteen months old, they were sitting at the table eating breakfast. Theresa's sister, Angie, was visiting. The baby was sitting in her high chair when she began waving towards the ceiling and saying 'hello!' and smiling all the while.

Theresa and Angie looked up, then at each other…then at the baby. They tried to get the baby's attention, but she was riveted on something unseen.

Finally, Theresa tapped her on the shoulder and said, 'Honey, who are you waving to?' She replied, 'Angels!'

At fifteen months old, Theresa had never told her daughter about angels, so it was not a word the child knew. Theresa and her sister burst into tears, knowing that the baby had indeed been entertained by angels. They wished they could see them too.

The Archangel Metatron works with children, especially those that are gifted spiritually. Another of his roles is to help children who have passed over to the other-side adjust themselves to their role as pure spirit once more.

Other angels protect our children physically. They step in front of cars and lift them out of danger. These stories are some of the most dramatic and unexplainable.

Katie's Guardian Angel

Sandy wrote to me about daughter Katie, who had an experience the whole family will never forget.

It was a cold, rainy December night in Albertville, Alabama. Sandy had never been afraid of stormy weather and neither had her husband. Their calm regard of Mother Nature had also been passed on to their three children.

That Friday night was no exception, with everyone going about their own business, despite the thunder and lightning that raged outside. Sandy's husband, Tim, was in the kitchen at about 7.00 p.m., making popcorn to snack on during the upcoming programme he planned to watch on television, while their two sons, Josh and Jake, eagerly awaited him in the living room.

Sandy's daughter, Katie, had decided to play in her room with her beloved dolls, and Sandy took the opportunity to read the newspaper in a rare moment of peace and quiet. All of a sudden, she heard a loud crash followed by Katie's faint screams for help. Jumping up and rushing into her room, she was appalled at the sight that she encountered. She told me that the memory of it would be etched in her memory for the rest of her life.

There on the floor lay her precious four-year-old baby girl under a massive solid oak antique wardrobe! She paused for just a second before screaming for Tim, who had not even heard the commotion from the other side of the house. Sandy knew that Katie's tiny body was probably crushed, and that there was no time to wait for help.

Without really thinking about her actions, she grabbed the heavy piece of furniture, and literally slung it off Katie and threw it to the other side of the room. Now, this might not be an incredible feat for some women, but for Sandy, it was astounding. By her own accounts, she is a small lady, weighing only 120 lbs (8½ stones). On that night, however, she was aware of what she called 'a helping hand' that helped her save her daughter.

She recalls kneeling down and gathering a frightened Katie up in her arms and holding her tight. They were both shaking when Tim and the boys made it into Katie's bedroom, a few seconds that had seemed like forever.

Sandy quickly explained in a quivering voice what had happened. They hardly seemed to believe that she was the one who had carelessly slung the large piece of furniture across the room, but no one could find any other explanation as to how it got there.

Tim knelt down beside Sandy and they began to examine Katie and try to determine the extent of her injuries. Even though they didn't see any blood on her, they assumed that her wounds were internal, and severe, due to the heavy weight that had fallen directly onto her tiny frame.

Tim and Sandy's oldest son, Josh, was the one who brought over the telephone, so that they could call the ambulance. It was when he announced that there was no dial tone (due to the storm) that Sandy really panicked. Katie was going to need medical attention and fast!

They realized that maybe they shouldn't move her, not knowing how badly she was hurt, but felt they had no other choice. The family said a silent prayer that God would watch over little Katie as they wrapped her in a small quilt, and Tim and the boys brought the car around to the back door.

For the whole family, the trip to the hospital seemed like a scene out of a horror movie. The storm was still raging all around. Lightning flashed in the sky above and the wind tried to blow them off the slippery road. Power lines were down on every side and they passed several cars stranded in ditches along the route. It was raining so hard that they could barely see the road ahead.

Under normal conditions, the hospital was only about a 20-minute drive, but it took Tim about an hour that evening. Josh and Jake thought Katie was dead, because she was so quiet, but Sandy kept her head close to hers and could feel her steadily breathing.

When the family finally made it to accident and emergency, the attendants rushed Katie straight into an examination room while Sandy hysterically relayed the details of the accident. Immediately, the doctor on duty began a full examination. Amazingly, he couldn't find a single scratch or bruise anywhere on her, but due to the severity of the accident, he ordered a full body x-ray.

Whilst all the tests were being carried out, Katie lay so still and peaceful that Sandy was sure she must be paralyzed. Within minutes, the results of the x-rays were delivered by the radiologist to the waiting crowd, who all studied them for several more minutes.

The doctor was now confused, and asked the family again if they were absolutely certain the piece of furniture had fallen directly on top of her?

To everyone's surprise, Katie sat up and answered him in her quiet little voice as her smile lit up the entire room. Katie explained to the doctor that the furniture had fallen right on top of her! She explained patiently how she was trying to climb up to the top and get her new doll when it just fell down on her. She said that she was scared, but it didn't 'smush' her because Angel Number 7 was holding it until Mummy got there!

The sceptical medical staff wanted to take more x-rays of little Katie's head after that, but, with tears in their eyes, the family picked up their little miracle and went home, where they still give thanks to Angel Number 7 who chose to visit them on that rainy night.

This story seems more than a miracle. We would be wise, however, to consider the words of St Augustine, who said, 'Miracles do not happen in contradiction to nature, but only in contradiction to that which is known to us of nature.'

Saved from a Dog Attack

Do angels drive cars? Maybe they do! This story comes from Ellie in America who says that when she was a child, she lived near a family that owned a large German shepherd guard dog.

The neighbourhood children were terrified of this huge dog, which was notoriously mean and would attack people. Ellie and her pals avoided walking past the house and devised creative routes away from the dog, including walking around the entire block to steer clear of him.

Even at a distance, they could hear the dog barking and growling.

One day, after Ellie had been out riding her bicycle, she headed home, walking down the opposite side of the street from where the dog lived. She heard the dog barking and snarling and glanced in the direction of the house.

She was horrified to see the animal charging towards her, the owner screaming at the dog to stop. It stampeded onward, and Ellie's heart thundered as she quickly placed her bicycle in front of her to block an attack.

When the dog reached the middle of the street, a car suddenly appeared, speeding up the hill and hit the dog. The dog was killed immediately, but when Ellie turned to see the car … it was gone! She is certain it was driven by an angel.

Not everything in the world is known to us after all…

Mothers know that their babies are looked after by angels. Angels stand watch over babies' cribs at night. If you peek in on your child when they laugh and giggle, they often seem to be playing with someone who isn't there. Or are they? Maybe babies see their guardian angels, just as Katie did.

Angels are looking out for sick children too.

Dina's granddaughter Nicki was sleeping. It was a worry because she had been sick a lot, but when Dina's daughter went to check on Nicki she was astounded to see an angel leaning over the bed. The angel was a child with golden curls. Dina told me the angel was just standing, keeping a watch over the baby.

Allison from America shares this incredible story that happened to her many years ago, when she was a newly divorced single mother. Allison had moved into a tiny apartment with her three-year-old son and six-month-old little girl named Tara. Times were tough and money was short. Her phone service had been cut off the week before because she hadn't paid the bill. To top it off, her car was not running…

One night, Tara awoke with a fever. Allison had no medicine to treat the child, and as the night wore on, Tara's fever raged. The mother's heart pounded with worry, and she wished she could call her friend to take them to the hospital. She sat at the table in desperation and suddenly her eyes were drawn to her phone.

She scoffed, knowing the phone was not in service. But something urged her to pick up the receiver. She was shocked to hear a dial tone! She quickly called a friend who hurried Allison and Tara to the hospital. When they returned home, the phone was dead again. Allison knows an angel got that phone working and will be forever grateful.

Angels have been known to assist with trauma in the extreme. Although they are not usually permitted to interfere with our life lessons, sometimes things do not always go according to plan. It is in cases such as these that angels are able to come along and lessen the pain a little. Sometimes they seem to change the original outcome.

One lady sent me an email to explain how the angels literally lifted her away from the pain, both physical and mental, by taking her spirit and lifting it out of her body completely. This is a not-unknown phenomenon but seems to happen most often when someone is in an accident. The experience is a little like the early stages of a near-death experience where the spirit and the physical body separate for a short while. In cases of abuse, it is as if the person is dying a little inside, so perhaps the affects of trauma are much the same. Often children do report that they were protected by angels at the time of such incidents.

Saving a Life, Protecting a Soul

Eileen is keen to spread the message so that others might be comforted. Eileen's angels stayed around for a lot longer though and helped her on many other occasions too.

Eileen lives in Hamilton, Ontario. She wrote to me because she wanted to share the amazing healing the angels gave her when she was molested as a child. The trauma started at the age of four. But she was not physically in her body when it happened.

Eileen told me that as soon as the physical trauma to her body began she was lifted up above her body. Angels would come and talk to her and tell her what was happening to her body below. They told her that her spirit was safe with them and that none of what was happening to her was her fault.

This powerful experience has compelled Eileen to tell others about how they can survive and overcome obstacles in life with faith. She wants people to be inspired by what happened to her rather than to feel sorry for her. She wants people to believe that angels exist and that they can help us in our daily lives. Even though the angels cannot be seen with our eyes, or touched with our hands, they still exist.

Her mother always told her she had a guardian angel, and that if she ever found herself in trouble, and her mother was not around, she was to ask her guardian angel for help. Being young and innocent Eileen never questioned that she did not have one, and just took it as fact that she did. I think this is often the key with younger children. They see angels because they don't know that they can't!

Eileen recalled another experience, which happened when she was five years old. It was early June on what she thought was a good day for swimming in the river. But when she asked her mother if she could go, her mother refused. Eileen suffered with bronchitis and the wind was just too cold that day. Eileen told me that she always got sick if she went swimming too early in the year.

Five-year-olds do not normally listen to reason. Eileen said that she wanted to prove her mother wrong and that she felt she would be perfectly well if she swam that day – which she wanted to do really badly.

Eileen decided to take a swim anyway, but instead of the river she chose the large trough down at the barn, which the animals drank from. At the time she wasn't bothered how dirty and disgusting the water was, she just wanted to get wet and prove to her mother that she would not get sick.

To her surprise the water was warm and felt good on her skin. There was only about two feet of water in the tub, which was why it felt so warm. Eileen stayed and played for around 20 minutes, after which she realized she was unable to climb out.

Every time she went to stand up, the wind, which was really cold, would put her right back in the warm water. She began to get upset and started to cry for her mother, when she remembered what her mother told her about her guardian angel: if she was ever in trouble her guardian angel would help.

Eileen remembers that she called several time aloud for her guardian angel to go and fetch her mother, and, amazingly, when she looked up, her mother was running out of the house, down to the barn, with a towel in her hand.

Eileen's mother was very angry with Eileen for disobeying her but when she was safe and dry, Eileen asked her mother how she knew that she had needed help. Eileen's mother explained that she had felt an overwhelming sense of urgency: she just knew her daughter needed her!

Our guardian angels are always around us – Eileen knows!

Saved From a Fall

I have received many exciting angel stories from the United States. Yes, the angel phenomenon is global and experienced by all cultures in every corner of the world. Tammy wrote to tell me about an incident that happened to her when she was seven years old.

What happened on this strange night? Did two children share a dream? It seems unlikely, so the only explanation seems to be that some unseen force was involved in this little incident. What would have happened to Tammy if something had not intervened? Could this have been something more serious if she had banged her head hard? Judge for yourself.

Tammy was asleep one night when she felt herself starting to roll off her bed. She woke up suddenly and braced herself for a hard landing on the floor. Instead, her body stopped in mid-air, as if soft arms caught her. All of a sudden, she was lifted up over her bed.

'I didn't feel any actual hands holding me,' Tammy said. 'But I opened my eyes and saw my little sister standing in my doorway.' She squeezed her eyes shut again as she was laid, gently, on the bed and immediately went back to sleep.

The next morning, Tammy was unsure if she had dreamed the amazing event. At breakfast, her little sister Amber said, 'Tammy, I saw you floating over your bed last night!'

Amber had heard a loud bang in Tammy's room the night before and scurried in to check on her sister. That's when she saw Tammy floating above the bed. She did not see anyone holding her up, but felt a wondrous calm melt over her as Tammy was placed back on the bed.

Tammy thinks she must have hit her head on the table beside her bed, which created the loud bang that Amber heard. As she was falling, an angel kept her safe. That was fifteen years ago, and Tammy and Amber still marvel over their incredible angel story.

12

Angels Helping in Times of Danger

Angels Helping in Times of Danger

ANGELS AS GUARDIANS

'Four Angels to my bed, Four Angels round my head,
One to watch and one to pray, And two to bear my soul away.'

THOMAS ADY, SEVENTEENTH-CENTURY ENGLISH WRITER

I firmly believe that we come to the Earth with a plan of lessons to learn.
I think of the Earth as a big classroom, but that doesn't mean that death is
always planned. I believe our angels can help to protect us when it is not
'our time'. Many of the appearances of angels seem to come during times
of great danger. The best way to illustrate how angels help us is to bring
you some of the amazing stories that people have sent me from all over
the world.

Leslie's story is one of these.

Angel on a Moped

Leslie lives in Cyprus and believes the island to be a very spiritual place. One particular day, when Leslie was driving to work on a little moped, she had a frightening experience.

'I was a holiday rep and so would often work late into the night. On this particular night, it was 10.00 p.m. when suddenly a car came out of a side turning right across me. I couldn't stop in time, and I remember thinking, I'm going to die.

The impact happened as I crashed into the side of the car. As I went through the air I was amazed to feel hands all down the length of my body! When I opened my eyes I was lying on my back, in a straight line on the roof of the car. I couldn't have been any closer to the edge, without falling off in fact. When I looked over I saw my moped crushed on the ground. It had flown right over the top of me and kept on going! The bike was a complete mess but I was fine.

I believed I was saved by angels who put out their hands to stop me. I remember the ambulance driver telling me that when he saw me lying on the car roof, he thought I was dead, because he couldn't see any way that I could have survived.

Since then I've had an angel dream. When I saw my angel, he was beautiful, with huge wings, and told me his name was Peter. Since then I often talk to him and ask for protection, never forgetting to say thank you.'

'See, I am sending an angel ahead of you to guard you along the way and to bring you to the place I have prepared.'

EXODUS 23:20

Angel Warning

Angels appear a lot when people are in vehicles. Emilie heard her life-saving instructions loud and clear:

When Emilie, from New York, was 18, she felt an odd foreboding as she left for work one afternoon. She gripped the steering wheel and took extra precautions as she drove down the highway, which was in places just a hilly gravel road with ditches on both sides.

Without warning, she lost control. Her car skidded on the gravel and became airborne. Emilie shouted, 'God, forgive me!' as the car flew off the road towards the top of a tree.

That's when she heard a woman's voice loud and clear. 'Lie down!' it directed.

Emilie let go of the steering wheel and lay down on the seat. Before she could cover her face, the windscreen shattered and shards of glass sprinkled over her body. She covered the back of her head as the car slammed into the wall of the ditch.

The car top was crushed and now lay against Emilie's body, yet she had no injuries. Emilie now firmly believes in God and his miracle angels.

This next story would fit well into several sections of this book. It appears that the angel in white was a little different from the angels people normally describe yet there seems little doubt that it was an angel just the same.

Yes, You have Angels in Your Life

Ellen wrote to tell me about a time when she was eight and her sister Betty picked her up from school.

Ellen was excited to show Betty her new bracelet she had received that day. She pulled it out of her backpack so quickly it flew out the window!

Ellen was frantic, as her parents had so lovingly bought the bracelet for her and she hadn't even worn it yet. She pleaded with Betty to turn the car round and help her find it. The road was quiet with no other cars in sight, so Betty reversed up to the place where they thought they lost the bracelet.

Ellen jumped out of the car and began her search, only to look up and see a white car speeding towards her. She heard her sister scream. 'At that very moment, someone grabbed me by the shoulders from the front and pushed me out of the way,' Ellen said. 'I fell to the ground, and could see my sister sobbing in the car.'

The white car pulled over and a young man dressed in a white shirt got out. He calmly asked if she was okay. When Ellen answered yes, he got back in the car and both he and the vehicle disappeared!

'Both my sister and I were flabbergasted,' Ellen said. 'It's been twenty-three years since that happened and I still believe he was an angel trying to get my attention. Letting me know I will always be protected.'

Sometimes angels will bring an urgent message to us – which seems particularly strong where loved ones are involved. Doris wrote to tell me about her experience.

Gut Instinct

'When my oldest daughter was only fifteen, she begged me to let her go to the drive-in with a friend and her cousin. I didn't want her to but she begged and pleaded, so I relented.

Later that evening I felt as if some unseen fist had knocked the breath out of me by hitting my stomach. I was worried but I didn't know why. I paced the floor and suddenly I realized that it must have something to do with my daughter. I started to get in my car to go and look for her, but my husband (who by this time thought I'd lost my mind) talked me out of it. He said that even if something was the matter, then she probably wouldn't be at the drive-in.

All of a sudden I had the overwhelming desire to pray. My mother-in-law went outside with me, and we both got on our knees on the patio, *praying to God that whatever was wrong, please spare our loved ones and bring them home safe.*

Soon a phone call came … from my daughter. They had been to fetch some beer and there had been an accident. Would I come and get her? She said no one was hurt except for her cousin, who had scraped her elbow.

When I arrived at the crash site, a state trooper was there, shaking his head. I couldn't see the car right away. It was down in a ravine. When I focused on it, I was as stunned as the trooper. The car was totally smashed with the top compressed inside … right down inside!

The trooper looked at me and said, "I've been a State Trooper for years. I have never seen all the occupants of a wreck like this walk away. I just don't think they are telling me the truth, but I don't know what else to believe."

If I wasn't sure about Guardian Angels before, I certainly was after that night. I wholeheartedly feel that her angel came to me with such urgency, I felt as if the breath had been knocked out of me. Jesus promised, "Where two or more are gathered together in my name, there I am also."

The two or more were myself, and my mother-in-law, and I also think my husband was silently praying, because he had never seen me like this before!'

~~~~

Not all danger comes in the form of an accident. And sometimes the danger is not apparent straight away. Danger can be many things that we are not aware of, or never know about.

You know those occasions when you decide out of the blue to drive to work a different way, after taking the same route for the last two years? Later on you discover there was a serious accident on the road you usually take to work, and it happened at the time you would normally have reached that stretch of road.

When I first started collecting angel stories a mother wrote to tell me that she had the strongest feeling her two-year-old son was in danger, even though she had left him safely watching television in the other room. She felt this nagging in her head, which she could not ignore, and following her instincts she rushed into the room only to discover that her son had disappeared. She was gripped with panic when she discovered that the front door was wide open. She rushed out of the door to see her son walking down the path, in the direction of the busy road ahead. She rushed down the drive and called him back. Can you imagine what might have happened?

There is a strange incident of my own which I could never explain. I remember one night when I was sitting in my car outside a supermarket when I had the strongest urge to lock my door. I began to panic, as I felt that someone was going to try and open the door. Moments later someone knocked loudly on the window and pushed down on the door handle – which of course was now locked. I let out a scream and heard the person outside laugh with glee! Turning crossly, I realized that the 'window knocker' was the son of a friend of mine – a nice guy whose intention had been to frighten me as a prank! Had I picked up the energy of his thoughts?

How do these messages reach us and why? Is this what we call our 'natural instinct'? Perhaps our angel voices *are* the 'natural instinct'. Is this inner knowing or strong feeling how we receive information, guidance and protection from our spiritual helpers and angels? It would certainly explain a lot of things!

Do we always make sensible decisions? No! Often we are not aware of the danger we put ourselves in until it is almost too late. We make a dumb decision – but we just don't realize it at the time! I'm not sure any of us are totally immune to this one!

Pearl found herself in danger of a different sort. It was one of those occasions where things just got a little out-of-hand. I'll let Pearl tell the story herself:

'The year was 1976 and my parents ran a gas station near the American border. My cousin Louis was coming to visit from California, and I met him at the airport. We stayed several days in my home town of Anchorage, when I asked him if he would like to hitch-hike to see my parents. I figured it would only take a whole day. Plus, I knew my parents would really like to see Louis.

We started out early and got about a hundred miles out of town. All we had with us were sleeping bags and a small amount of cash (about

$10.00). Although in my defence, I have to say that we were only 17–18 years old at the time, and not real smart!

We only got one ride later that day and spent the night sleeping on the side of the road. The next day we didn't get a ride at all. No one would pick us up! After three days, we were stranded, and walking, trying to get to somewhere we could make a phone call.

In all that time, we didn't have a thing to eat. Needless to say, we were very hungry and when we found a porcupine walking along the road, we started discussing ways to turn him into our dinner! Of course, all the while he's looking over his shoulder at us, but we didn't have the heart to really hurt him!

After walking a few more miles we sat and rested, it was so bright and beautiful out. As I looked over at the trees I said jokingly to my cousin, wouldn't it be great if all those pine trees were apple trees? Just then, it started to rain, so we ran a few feet to a nearby bridge so that we could shelter under it. Rather bizarrely, on our way down the bank we found a new-looking paper bag, which we grabbed to open under the bridge. Imagine how stunned we were when we opened up the bag. Inside there were two perfectly good apples!

We had both agreed that we had prayed for food, and I think God sent an angel to deliver it.

It stopped raining almost immediately and no more than 10 minutes later we got a ride all the way to Tok, where my parents lived. It's strange how there wasn't a cloud in the sky before it rained … it made me wonder.'

Can angels actually touch us or even catch us? I think that they can. I can't image how difficult this might be for them but it does happen from time to time. During my research I read some amazing stories of people being held by angels … and pulled, caught and lifted! Tracking down the original source for such stories is very difficult but I found this experience, sent to me by Claire, to be similar to some of these.

Claire wrote to me because she felt that, try as she might, she was unable to get a sign from her angels that they were around. She added this experience to the email as a 'by the way, it's probably nothing but…' comment at the end!

I think her angels are around and making themselves very well known indeed! Sometimes we just miss the obvious!

'...I've also had other experiences. I cannot be sure but I believe I may have had a guardian angel save my life.

Years ago I was trying to cross a very busy road where the cars would speed by very fast. A car was parked by the side and I couldn't see well, but I decided to go for it anyway and went to run across the road, when I felt someone pull me back. A car swerved and missed me by inches, but when I turned there was no one around me!'

13

Angels —
How We Can
Help Them

Angels —
How We Can Help Them

HUMANS AS 'ANGELS'?

Do angels need help? Yes, of course they do! They often inspire us to help pass on important information for them. Strangers we meet in the park while feeding the ducks can give us the most profound insight to a problem! I bet if you were to meet them again they wouldn't even remember that little phrase they told you which changed the whole direction of your life. But this sort of thing happens all the time.

I tried to think of some incidents in my own life. There were many occasions where I have felt 'compelled' to help someone in a small way, and I firmly believe that the other peoples' angels were asking me to pass on information or offer practical help on their behalf.

I remember once two ladies whose car had broken down by the side of the road. Now normally I wouldn't stop for anyone, as I'm well aware of the dangers of picking up hitchhikers! But this was different and I felt compelled to pick them up. I actually drove them home (a village just a few miles away) and when they offered me compensation I think I muttered something surreal like, 'just do the same favour for someone else one day!' Am I an angel? Honestly no! I'm just as good and as indifferent as everyone else, but after this little experience I felt amazing inside for days! Was this my angelic reward?

We all do these little things on occasion. Isn't it fun to do a stranger a little favour and then to walk away quietly into the night! Perhaps we are all 'angels in disguise' – if we want to be…

Angels don't own a body and sometimes it is easier for them to borrow ours. This is not in any way a scary thing. They use us as a type of telephone and pass a message to us which, when it arrives, just seems like 'an idea of our own'. Sometimes we have an urge to do an act of kindness and we don't know why this happens!

Here is another, rather stranger example of my own.

I used to live on a busy main road, which backed onto a corn field in a beautiful English village. To the left of the field ran the playing fields of our village school and I would regularly look out of my daughter's bedroom window and despair at the rubbish which had gathered behind the school fence.

On this one particular day I felt the urge to go and clean it up. Now don't get me wrong – I don't like cleaning and this was totally out of character! The urge was so strong that I almost argued with myself about going. It was a miserable day and I figured that I could wait until the weather was better, but despite my misgivings, I fetched a plasticized apron and a pair of rubber gloves. Then I sorted out a strong rubbish bag and left the house. It was raining and I cursed my way across the field but I could not stop. I was a woman on a mission.

I decided that I would pick up a few pieces of rubbish closest to the house and then go in. It was raining after all. I soon cleared up all the crisp packets and drink cartons behind the house and started working my way up the field. Even though I was cleaning community rubbish I was not feeling very charitable at all. I moaned to myself as I got closer to the school, but I could not stop myself. I began walking the length of the school fence, all the while thinking that I would just do a little more. But I picked up everything! I cleared every little piece of rubbish from that field!

Feeling satisfied, I stood up to survey my work. At that very moment, the sun came out from behind a cloud, and a beam of sunlight directly shone on the area I had been working on. I looked to my right to where

I heard a rustle, and noticed a little bird had flown down and perched on an ear of corn. He was so close that I could have reached out and touched him. A snapping sound under the crops drew my attention and a baby rabbit jumped out onto the path in front of me! It was like something out of a surreal movie.

Butterflies and bees began to fly and buzz around me and I walked home in a bit of a daze! I knew that something extraordinary had happened that day and I felt that my nature visitors had come to say thanks!

Like before, I felt fantastic for days afterwards, and yet I had been pretty moody about getting out in the field in the first place. I think that it was a little job that needed doing and as I lived so close, why shouldn't it have been me that took on the job?

There have been other occasions when I have felt drawn to follow an action. Have you ever bought flowers for people you don't know very well? Do you make a point of chatting to people in the supermarket queue?

A Lesson in Kindness

I use my local village shop almost every day. Some days I call in several times throughout the day and it is always packed with other village shoppers. On this one particular day I spotted a retired lady in front of me in the queue buying her shopping, which was nothing unusual in itself. What was different is that I had the strongest urge to start up a conversation with her.

I am quite a confident person but even so, I did not know this lady, and had no idea what to say to her. The urge to chat to this complete stranger was so great I just started muttering something about the weather with a strange smile on my face. Amazingly she did not run out of the shop in fright but seemed keen to chat back.

She paid for her shopping and we continued to talk as I, in turn, paid for my own items. Then we stood talking for several minutes more. As she turned around to leave, she said to me, 'Thanks for the chat. I live on my own and apart from the lady at the till, you are the only person I have spoken to all week!'

As you can imagine, I felt very humbled by the experience and thanked my angels for the opportunity to have spoken to this lovely lady. I decided there and then that embarrassment is not a good enough reason not to talk to someone. We never know when a few kind words can make a big difference in another person's life.

If we knew this sort of information in advance, would it make a difference to the way we dealt with someone in everyday life? When your boss becomes very irritable one week, would we show them some compassion if we knew a close family friend was dying? When the shop assistant snaps at you for no apparent reason would we show more tolerance if we knew their beloved dog had recently been run-over? If we noticed a mum at the school gates looking scruffy and unkempt would we stop to say hello if we realized her husband had just left her?

Driving Vision Angels

There are some mysteries where it is difficult to decide if the helpful visitor is an angel or not. Were these angels or men acting on their angelic instinct, or angels in the guise of men?

Teresa of Ontario, Canada, is certain an angel saved her life. Back in the autumn of 1997, she was speeding along the road on her way home from a night class. It was raining lightly, with no other cars in sight.

She was listening to some spiritual music to help her relax when suddenly she felt a hand touch her right shoulder. A clear vision unfolded before her. Teresa saw herself lose control of the car and flip over. The accident scene was laid out before her, then the headlines in the next day's newspaper, she even watched her own funeral.

The vision stretched into the future showing her parents' pain, and she heard friends talking about her and how they missed her.

Teresa's body shuddered with chills that stretched down into her toes. Immediately, she turned off the music and slowed down. She heard a loud bang and slowly pulled over to the side of the road and stopped.

Out of nowhere, two men in a tow truck pulled over and offered to help. They found three large holes in her front tyre and shook their heads. 'If you had been going any faster, you would be dead,' they declared.

Teresa was flabbergasted, and grateful for the angel who had warned her so she could avoid an early death.

We don't always have this knowledge, but the angels do. Tolerance, compassion and kindness are important lessons and by opening ourselves to the wider picture we can help others, and even feel better in ourselves. Who would have thought that picking up rubbish would have made me feel so great … once I'd got over my lazy reservations!

ANGELS DISGUISED AS ANIMALS?

Do angels work with animals to create healing and life-saving opportunities? I believe they can do this too. There are many amazing stories of animals saving the lives of humans. Sometimes these animals love and care for the people they save. Perhaps they and their owners lived together for a long time. These stories appear all over the world and sometimes the explanation is less clear, as in this story sent to me by Deborah.

'An ugly old grey cat came to my son's family's home one day – they wouldn't feed the old cat, hoping it would go back to wherever it came from. The cat had been there just a few days when my one-year-old granddaughter was swinging in a child's swing out in their yard. Everyone was sitting just a few feet away but never noticed the big copperhead snake crawling towards the baby – nobody but the old ugly cat!

Just a few inches from the baby's feet the old cat pounced on the snake, killing it quickly. The old cat was treated like royalty from then on – but he left as quietly as he came and they never saw him again.'

14

Angel Healing Stories

Angel Healing Stories

Amazing stories reach me of angel healing. This does seem an important role of the archangels in particular. Archangel Raphael in particular is an angel healer. Often in these many healing stories the angels arrive 'in the body of humans'.

This special story comes from John in Canada.

Nursing Angel

'On a Friday afternoon in 1980, my wife and I were in a devastating car accident. At the scene I was most concerned. I thought my wife was the most seriously injured, she was semi-conscious and I was walking about, talking to police and witnesses. I even asked one of the neighbourhood ladies for a drink of water, and I smoked my last cigarette ever.

When the ambulances arrived, they put my wife in one ambulance and the other driver and me in the second. I was sitting up in the passenger seat, talking to the attendant about some pain I had in my chest. He asked if I had a heart condition and the next thing I remembered was that they were giving me smelling salts. Apparently, I had fainted.

After I was taken to hospital, the pain increased and I was in extreme difficulty. From the Friday, right up until the Monday I remember very little. I had several blood transfusions and I have some memories of glimpses of doctors, family, priests and so on. I do remember that on the Monday morning the surgeon and consultant got into a heated discussion about how they should proceed with my treatment. As it turns out I was bleeding internally, but they didn't know where or from what. The surgeon won the day and it was decided that he would operate (at 1 p.m. on the Monday). As I went to surgery, I had the feeling that I might not make it, and I felt like it didn't matter…

After the surgery, I was taken to the Intensive Care Unit where I remained until the following Thursday. Throughout this time, I remember going in and out of awareness. Visits from my family, the doctors, the therapists…

One particular physiotherapist made me mad, as she was continually after me to breathe, breathe, deeper, deeper … Apparently, they had removed my spleen and repaired some other internal damage, but because I had been a heavy smoker, the lungs were filling with fluid and I needed to help expel it.

This is where I met my angel, she appeared to be like an old lady and she sat in the corner of my ICU room as long as I remained there. Whenever I was letting up on my breathing she would remind me what the therapist had said. Continually, over three or four days she was always there, day and night, cajoling me to keep going and not give up on my breathing.

After I left the ICU, I started to slowly improve. It was about 18 months before I had regained my health. I know the person in my room was my angel or 'the angel' that was sent to help me through. I saw her and I heard her but no one else did. I often think of her and wish I could see her more clearly – it's a fuzzy memory, and I didn't ever see my angel again.'

Let's hope that John doesn't need to see his angel again! It does make you wonder why we are able to see our angels when we are seriously ill as John was here. I surmise that it may be because 'we' are closer to their world (being closer to death and in and out of consciousness), making it easier for them to reach down to our world! Maybe it is only during great distress that we actually *need* to see them!

An Angel Kept Me on My Life Path

Cathy from Washington in America was drawn to healing. Even as a child, she felt this calling, and learned an energy healing system called Reiki. But after many losses and personal frustrations, she gave it up and lost her way.

Everything seemed to be going wrong until one night she was lying in bed watching television when she felt a tap on her shoulder. She turned around, but nobody was there. Then she noticed a tall figure with wings looming in front of the television.

He spoke softly, urging Cathy not to give up, that she had work to do. Cathy's faith was instantly restored, and she began working with Reiki energy again. She knew it was her calling … her destiny.

The night her brother died of Lou Gehrig's disease (amyotrophic lateral sclerosis), she was visited by an angel again, this time in her dreams. Cathy now relies on angels and calls them to her when she is struggling. They have not let her down.

In this next story, Diane seems to have had an out-of-body experience when she saw what, she now realizes, was an angel.

In the Arms of an Angel

Diane from Iowa went to see a therapist after suffering a series of panic attacks and shooting pains throughout her body. The doctor talked her back to the memory of a car accident her mother told her about years before.

She remembered her mother saying Diane was just two years old, and playing roughly with her two sisters in the back seat of the car while her mother drove along. Without warning, the car door flew open, and Diane tumbled from the car. As she bounced along the pavement, her flesh was scraped from her body and the hair ripped from her scalp.

Later at the hospital, doctors found a skull fracture and tried to stitch up her many wounds. The story was startling for Diane. Her earliest memory of childhood was of a car wheel coming towards her head.

The next thing she saw was the back of her mother's head. A man with a hat and coat was driving their car and Diane was lying on a pillow on her mother's lap. It didn't occur to Diane for years that she was seeing this from the back seat of the car.

Her mother was sobbing and Diane wanted to soothe her, when suddenly she was shifted to another place. A beautiful lady was cradling Diane in her arms, cooing her. The features are vague, but she remembers the colours gold, white and blue. Diane was frightened of her mother's tears, but the lady told her not to be afraid and all would be fine.

Once Diane realized this woman was an angel who helped her through the terrifying accident when she was a child, the panic attacks went away forever.

15

Guided Angel Meditations

Guided Angel Meditations

(See also Candles, Crystals and Herbs, page 255, for more on meditation and prayer work with candles and meeting the crystal angels.)

WHAT IS A GUIDED MEDITATION?

A guided meditation is just exactly what it says. Rather than letting your mind concentrate on nothing, or one single thing (like a candle flame or a flower), a guided meditation talks you through a journey.

This journey usually starts with simple relaxation, which can involve breathing techniques, or sometimes a 'voice-over' (your own, if you are pre-recording your meditation), reminding you to relax your body a little at a time.

Next you go on your 'journey', which may be to a place to meet your angel, chat to your angel or a place you can work with your angel.

Lastly you end your journey and return 'home', coming back into the room. Remember this is a relaxing meditation. You are not in a trance! You are totally in control at all times and even though, with practice, you can become very relaxed (and may even fall asleep – although this is not the object of the meditation), you can open your eyes and end the meditation at any time.

If you have never meditated before then a 'guided' meditation, with a voice to lead you through the various steps, is a good way to start off. The hardest part about meditation of any sort is keeping your 'mind on the topic!' Once we start to relax, all those 'pressing' little jobs that you have been putting on hold will begin to drop into your mind! '…must buy sugar…haven't rang Janice yet…pick up the dry cleaning!' Just acknowledge them and let the thought float on by before carrying on with the meditation.

Start off with a simple meditation. Just relax for a couple of minutes. Build up to a longer meditation of five, ten, fifteen or twenty minutes. Before you know it, you will be happy to sit for a whole hour! (If only we had the time, what with all the sugar we have to buy and dry cleaning we have to pick up!)

You can memorize the meditation, or ask a friend to read it for you, or tape yourself reading the meditation and play it back.

The angel 'loving energy' meditation below is a good one to start with, and it is only short so you can memorize it. Have a go!

GETTING READY FOR MEDITATION

First find a comfortable place to sit or lie. Make sure you will not be disturbed, and perhaps switch off the phone. Play some gentle and relaxing music if you wish.

Sometimes during meditation your body temperature can drop a little, so make sure you don't get cold. Turn up the heating a little bit, keep a blanket handy or put on a pair of warm socks.

Angels can help with all sorts of ventures. You can choose an archangel to help you (by picking an angel that has the specific skills for the job) or just do a general meditation asking for 'the right angel' to help you. Meditation is a wonderful way of getting close to your angels and to ask them for any help you need. In meditation, our energy vibration is raised a little, making us a little closer to the angel's realm.

ANGEL 'LOVING ENERGY' MEDITATION

Ready
Follow the meditation preparation suggested above.

Steady
When you are ready to begin, place your hands in your lap or by your side if you are lying down.

Go
Close your eyes, and relax. Take three deep breaths, breathing in through your nose and blowing the breath out through your mouth.

Imagine yourself surrounded by a white fluffy cloud. Puff the cloud out until you can imagine it surrounding your whole body in an egg shape. This cloud is bouncy and soft.

[If you can't easily see the cloud, just know that it is there.]

Now see this cloud of energy turning a soft pink colour. This beautiful pink cloud is full of loving energy. You are surrounded by love.

...you feel safe, warm and comfortable. You are surrounded by love. You are surrounded by love and hugged by your angels. Feel this energy as a cloud of angel love.

Next let this cloud of loving energy enter through the top of your head and flood down through your body. Feel this loving energy enter every part of you, inside and out. As the love moves into each part of your body, let it replace any negative or uncomfortable energy that gets in its way. This negative energy just dissolves and is easily replaced with the pink energy. As it reaches each and every part of your body, know that it makes you feel healthy and happy. This energy will lift your spirits and make you feel glad to be alive in the world.

…you feel safe, warm and comfortable. You are surrounded by love. You are surrounded by love and filled with love both inside and out. Feel this energy as a gift of love from your angels.

Sit and enjoy this pink cloud of love for as long as you feel comfortable.

[If you are recording your voice, leave a few minutes space here, so that you can appreciate this feeling a while longer.]

When you are ready, take three deep breaths, breathing in through your nose and blowing out through your mouth. Bring your loving cloud of pink energy with you. You can keep this special energizing and loving cloud with you for as long as you need it.

Open your eyes and come back into the room.

[Sit and relax for a few minutes to get your bearings again. Have a warm drink and eat a biscuit or piece of fruit to ground yourself once again.]

MEET YOUR GUARDIAN ANGEL MEDITATION

Ready

Follow the meditation preparation suggested previously.

Steady

When you are ready to begin, place your hands in your lap or by your side if you are lying down.

Go

Close your eyes, and relax. Take three deep breaths, breathing in through your nose and blowing the breath out through your mouth.

Imagine a white light flooding down through the top of your head and flowing down through the centre of your body. See the white light filling every part of every limb.

Follow the light around the inside of your head, filling your jaws, flowing around your ears, the backs of your eyes, before flowing down into your neck and shoulders. As light fills each part of your body, you are feeling more and more relaxed. Any negativity or tension disappears as the light flows into that area.

Feel the light now flowing down into your arms, down through your elbows, your wrists, your hands and fingers. Feel the light flooding into this area. The whole of your arms now are relaxed and tension free. As the light moves down your body you are feeling more and more relaxed.

Feel the light now gathering in your chest, in your back and down through your stomach and flowing down to the base of your pelvis. Light is circulating into every space within your body. As the light moves down your body you are feeling more and more relaxed.

Feel the light now moving into your buttocks, your thighs, your knees, your calves, your ankles, your feet…your toes. Light is circulating into every space within your body. As the light moves down your body you are feeling more and more relaxed.

Feel the light now moving out the ends of your toes and flowing back up the outside of your body. The light is moving up to the top of your head. Your body is relaxed and comfortable on the inside and outside. You are safe and protected. Check the light is now in every part of your body. Seal the light around your body now. Feel the light fluffing up around you like a white protective blanket.

Take three more deep and cleansing breaths – slowly … in through your nose … blow the breath out through your mouth … again … in … blow out … one last time now and in … hold the breath and blow out … ahhhhhhh.

You are now ready to meet your angel.

You are safe and protect and feeling very relaxed now. In the distance you see a golden glow. This is your guardian angel, and when you are ready you can ask your angel to move close to you.

[Wait a few moments here before continuing with the exercise.]

Your guardian angel moves in a golden ball of light, which is filled with love – love for you. As the light moves nearer you can feel this love beginning to merge with the light which fills and surrounds you. Spend a few minutes absorbing this amazing feeling as your guardian angel draws close to your side.

[Wait a few moments here before continuing with the exercise.]

You have waited for this moment for a long time. Your angel is as excited to greet you as you are to meet them. Embrace for a few moments and feel their love pouring into your very being. You have so many questions, and while you hold your angel you can begin to prepare your questions.

[Wait a few moments here before continuing with the exercise.]

Now it is time. Ask if your angel is a male or a female energy. Ask them *now* and take your first instinct as the correct answer. If you did not hear the answer within your mind, believe that you *know* the answer.

Now it is time for the next question. Ask your angel their name. Ask them *now* and take your first instinct as the correct answer. If you did not hear the answer within your mind, believe that you *know* the answer. Your angel may have a traditional name or something more normal. Whatever name you hear is the right answer.

Your angel has a surprise for you … a special gift. Open this gift now and your angel will explain to you why they have chosen it for you.

[Wait a few moments here before continuing with the exercise.]

Thank your angel for their special gift. Now is the time for you to chat with your angel about any problems you might have in your life. Your angel can offer you loving support and guidance. Spend a few minutes now chatting with your angel.

[Wait a few moments here before continuing with the exercise.]

It is now time for your angel to leave. But remember that they are not really going anywhere. Your angel is with you always. Your angel is just a breath away and you can call on them to support you at any time. Know that if you want to talk to your angel you can meet them again at any time by sitting down in quiet contemplation and meditation. You can do this anywhere at any time.

Your angel takes you in a loving embrace one more time before they go. The golden light fills your aura before your angel blends back into the light behind them.

You are feeling happy and relaxed, calm and peaceful. Meeting your guardian angel is a wonderful experience. Each time you do this exercise the experience will get stronger and the link will become closer. In time you will need to just 'still your mind' to feel your angel's presence.

Now start to count backwards from 10 to 1. As you count down the numbers you will become more and more aware. Bringing your consciousness back into the room…

10 … moving back into the room … 9 … you are back in the room now … 8 … 7 … 6 … you can open your eyes now … 5 … 4 … 3 … open your eyes and wide awake … 2 … 1 … wide awake now … stretch and shake your arms.

[Sit and relax for a few minutes to get your bearings again. Have a warm drink and eat a biscuit or piece of fruit to ground yourself once again.]

When you are ready, go over in your mind what happened at your meeting and what your angel discussed with you. Referring to the Communicating With Your Angels chapter (page 281), write a few notes about your experiences in a special notebook if you wish.

16

Candles, Crystals and Herbs

Candles, Crystals and Herbs

CANDLE COLOURS AND ANGELS

Angels are often associated with a particular colour, and these colours can be used when communicating with your angels. Many people like to burn candles when meditating too, and you can use the chart on pages 258–60 with any angel candle rituals, prayers and angelic requests of your own.

If you have difficulty in finding any particular colour, a white candle can be used in its place. White is also used for cleansing and clearing, and you may wish to burn a white candle before any work with the higher realms. Use the chart as a guide, but if you feel strongly that another colour will work better for you in your situation – then always follow your own inner guidance and gut instincts. You are your own expert so trust yourself first of all.

Here are the candle colours that I normally use for my angel work.

CANDLE COLOUR	ASSOCIATED ANGELS AND ARCHANGELS	OTHER REFERENCES FOR THE COLOUR IN GENERAL USE
White	Uriel, All angels and higher realms	Use to replace all other colours. Used in space-clearing and cleansing sacred space. Also represents chastity and protection
Black	Archangel Michael	Strictly speaking – not a colour at all. Although many believe this 'colour' candle is traditionally used in black magic, a black candle is also used to banish evil and removing negative energy, which makes it perfect for protection
Gold	Archangel Metatron, Archangel Gabriel	Relating to the Sun and the element of air. Used in conjunction with protection requests, and developing children's spiritual gifts. Sometimes used to represent financial wealth, masculine and feminine energies.
Silver	Archangel Ariel, Archangel Gabriel and Archangel Haniel	In magical terms, silver is usually associated with the Moon and therefore moon cycles – a feminine energy
Red	Archangel Azrael, Archangel Michael	Sexual passion, lust and romantic love and therefore relating to the heart (both physical and spiritual). Connected to the element of fire, also to do with the blood, courage, energy and victory

CANDLE COLOUR	ASSOCIATED ANGELS AND ARCHANGELS	OTHER REFERENCES FOR THE COLOUR IN GENERAL USE
Blue	Archangel Ariel, Archangel Raphael and Archangel Michael	A spiritual colour, which is also used to bring the realms closer together (meeting between the two worlds). Perfect for studying and used to symbolize water. Also peace, wisdom and transformation
Green	Archangel Ariel, Archangel Haniel, Gabriel and Archangel Metatron	Used when working with romantic love energy. Also represents fertility and new life – so associated with spring and new plant growth. Also suggestive of spiritual healing and growth of spirit. Used to bring good luck and fortune
Yellow	Archangel Chamuel	Happiness, joy and freedom. Yellow represents anything which is full of life and vitality
Orange	Archangel Raguel	Perfect for mending and healing of relationships, fixing legal matters and monetary and material wealth. Often associated with children and childhood issues, and connected to careers
Brown	Archangel Chamuel, Archangel Uriel, Nature Spirits and Elementals	Associated with earth healing and connected to the animal kingdom. Friendship

Candle Colour	Associated Angels and Archangels	Other References for the Colour in General Use
Purple/Lilac	Archangel Haniel, Archangel Gabriel	A Traditional 'royal' colour. Usually associated with wealth, fame, wisdom, power and ambitions. Used for promoting and developing psychic gifts
Pink	Archangel Jophiel, Archangel Ariel, Archangel Jeremiel	Innocence and unconditional love. Family love rather than romantic relationships. Works with relaxation and honour as well as communication with friends and family

Preparing Candles for Use

Candles can be prepared for celestial use by dedicating the candle to your angel meditations. Normally, once dedicated, a candle is used for only the one purpose and afterwards is burnt down completely. If you are using your candle for short periods of time, you could wrap your candle after use and burn it again for the same purpose, or use smaller coloured tea-lights (safety candles) instead.

Holding the candle in both hands, you can ask the designated angel or archangel for permission to light the candle or to dedicate its use, using words or phrases that are relevant to you. You might say something like:

'Archangel [insert name of angel here], I dedicate this [state colour] candle to my meditation [or other use] and ask that you recognize and work with your perfect abilities to help me with my designated task. I ask all of this to be to the highest good of all concerned and working within God's holy light and love. Amen.'

Candles are used all around the world to represent the 'bringing in of the light' (the good, the God essence/creator). Candles are lit to open up communication and begin rituals, magical and religious ceremonies. Blowing out a candle is a symbolic way of closing and finishing your communication or prayer work, and you can do this at the end.

Suggested Ritual for Meditation Using Candles

♥ Choose a candle of a suitable colour for the archangel and purpose.

♥ Remember that white candles can be used to replace all other candle colours or for when no appropriate colour has been listed. Respect your own intuition if you feel drawn to a particular colour.

♥ Find or create a quiet space for meditation. You can cleanse your space using suggested herbs (see 'Herbs and Angels' page 266), by burning sage (in the form of smudge sticks), or perhaps by placing a few drops of rose or frankincense pure aromatherapy oils in water on the top of an oil burner.

♥ If you wish you can bring into your space a rose quartz crystal or other crystal chosen from the list in the next section.

♥ Place a bunch of flowers, a single stem or leaf, or perhaps a small potted plant into your space to welcome the natural energy into your meditation or prayer space.

♥ You can play relaxing or New Age-type angel music if you wish.

♥ Hold your candle and dedicate it to your ritual, using the words suggested above or create your own.

♥ Light the candle and place in a secure holder.

♥ Continue with your meditation or prayer to the designated angels or sit in meditation and contemplate your angels. Spend some time doing this – perhaps 20 minutes or half an hour. Take your time and enjoy the experience.

♥ After finishing your work, always remember to thank your angels for their help and blow out your candle, or leave it in a safe place to burn away completely.

You can thank your angel by saying the following words, or whatever you feel is appropriate:

'Archangel [add angel name here, or use the name of your own angel if you know it*], I thank you for your service and communication from the higher realms. I ask to be wrapped in your love and assistance. Working with the love of God and the highest good of all, and my own free will … I bless you. Amen.'

* You can find the name of your own angel by following the meditation in the Guided Angel Meditation chapter, page 245.

Note: Always remember that burning candles can be dangerous and that they should never be left untended.

CRYSTALS AND ANGELS

If you want to bring a particular angel energy close to you, then you might wish to work with crystal energy too. Many sources associate angels with the attributes of particular crystals. Here are some of them:

ANGEL	ASSOCIATED CRYSTALS
Ariel	Sodalite
Azrael	Amethyst
Chamuel	Amber (not actually a crystal but a tree resin)
Gabriel	Clear Quartz
Haniel	Red Jasper
Metatron	Beryl
Raphael	Rose Quartz
Uriel	Obsidian

Using Crystals with Angels

You can use crystals in many ways.

- ❤ If you are working with a specific angel already, you may wish to carry around the associated crystal to act as a reminder of the angel energy you are bringing close to you.

- ❤ You can place the crystal next to your chosen angel divination card (see the section relating to working with angel divination cards, page 301).

- ❤ For meditation. Hold the crystal during your meditation, while concentrating on the qualities of the angel.

- ❤ Wear your crystal as a piece of jewellery for the same purpose.

Other Angel-related Crystals

CRYSTAL NAME	MEANINGS AND USES
Angel Wing Agate	Displays a structure with a 'wing-like' tube appearance. Sometimes used to help bring a serene life of no worries. Believed to act as a doorway to contact with other planes of existence.
Angelite	A blue and white crystal. Helps with spiritual journeys and off-world communication. Symbol of light and of love.
Celestite	Found in blue, white, yellow orange, red and red-brown. Helps transfer information from the angelic realms.
Clear Quartz	As with white candles, clear quartz is the 'all singing, all dancing' crystal which can be used for most things. Clear quartz is a perfect angel meditation crystal.
Goethite	Scales of crystal form this prismatic crystal, which can assist in communication with the angels.

CRYSTAL NAME	MEANINGS AND USES
Lapis Lazuli	Legend tells us that this blue stone was used by King Solomon (a great crystal wearer). An angel helped Solomon control the many demons (who assisted in the building of his temple) by wearing a special ring.
Lepidocrocite	This crystal ranges in colour from yellow through to red. Used with amethyst (or quartz), it can also be used to enhance contact with the angelic realm
Petalite	This can be white, grey, white with a tinge of red and white with a tinge of green. It has been called the 'stone of the angels', and is used to help bring you closer to the angels
Quartz with Caledonite	Quartz with a greenish tinge (not chlorite, which also gives this colouration). Associated with pure contact from the angels
Rose Quartz	A gentle loving and healing stone which is perfect for angel meditation and prayers

One of the most ancient of beliefs is that every aspect of nature, each living thing and every plant, animal and even inanimate objects, such as mountains, have their own spirit energy. Victorian painters actually drew flowers with their accompanying fairy or nature spirits; woodlands have their elves and gnomes, and even crystals themselves are said to contain an angel inside their structure.

Crystal Meditation

A meditation to meet your crystal angel:

♥ Choose a crystal. You can pick a crystal from the list previously, or use one which you are particularly drawn to.

♥ Find or create a quiet space for your meditation. As with all meditation, you can cleanse your space using herbs (see 'Herbs and Angels' page 266), by burning sage (in the form of smudge sticks), or perhaps placing a few drops of rose or frankincense pure aromatherapy oils in water on the top of an oil burner.

♥ You can bring other natural things such as flowers or plants into your meditation space if you wish.

♥ Play relaxing or New Age-type angel or classical music if you wish.

♥ Sit in a comfortable high-backed chair, or lie down in a warm, comfortable space.

♥ Hold your crystal in both hands and breathe in and out slowly and deeply.

Begin your ritual by taking three or four deep breaths. Breathe in through your nose and hold for the count of three before blowing the breath out again through your mouth.

Imagine yourself surrounded by pink light. Feel this light surround you like a pink bubble or cloud. This pink light is full of love. Imagine this pink light flowing through you and through and around your crystal.

Now imagine the crystal growing in size; you are able now to walk and float around the outside of the crystal and explore every single angle and side of this beautiful creation. Spend time getting to know your crystal. Feel its wonderful energy and soak up the loving energy that it is sending you.

Continue breathing slowly and deeply, all the while enjoying the energy of this loving stone.

After a while, a doorway opens up to the centre of the crystal. The energy is welcoming and the angel of the crystal is waiting inside to communicate with you. You can go inside now and explore further.

From the inside the crystal is filled with light and the angel is waiting to embrace you with her love. As the angel of the crystal touches your energy body, all the positive energy fills your very being and the angel tells you her name.

The angel spends time with you, and shares the secrets of being at one with the crystal. You may remember some of this information when you leave or you may retain this information on a higher level of consciousness.

Relax and enjoy being in this light and loving space with the angel of the crystal, and when you are ready you just leave the same way that you came in. The entrance is well lit, and remains open the whole time.

Take a few more deep breaths and, as you look at the crystal from the outside once again, feel the crystal shrinking back to its original size. You may keep the loving feelings and messages from the crystal for as long as you wish.

Know that you can go back at any time and communicate with the angel of the crystal or any other crystal of your choosing.

When you are ready, open you eyes and bring yourself back into the room. Sit for a few minutes relaxing. After finishing your meditation, always remember to thank the angel for her help.

Ground yourself back in the earth world by having something to eat or drink afterwards.

HERBS AND ANGELS

There is an 'Angel of Herbs' mentioned in the 'Alphabet of Rabbi Akiba'. It is included amongst the '…splendid, terrible, and mighty angel chiefs' who passed before God extolling and rejoicing in the first Sabbath! Sadly we do not have a name for this angel, but it is interesting that the subject was considered important enough to have its own guardian.

There are many herbs and plants associated with angels. Here are a few of them.

HERB/PLANT/OILS	USES
Angelica *Angelica archangelica* *'The herb of the angels'*	Angelica, a member of the parsley family, is a plant native to northern Europe and Asia, which blooms in the spring There is a legend that says that in 1665, a group of monks were dying of the plague. The angels came in a dream to one of the monks and told them to eat angelica. Immediately they had chewed the plant, they were cured In ancient times, angelica was used to ward off evil spirits
Frankincense *Boswella carterii*	Called 'food for the Gods', this oil is suggested to be useful for raising the energy in a place where angel contact is required (it keeps negative entities at bay) Can be used in an oil burner – add two or three drops to water in the top of your burner, or use as incense
Rose	The scent of roses is often associated with angels. Many people smell a rose scent when an angel has appeared in a visitation
Vanilla	The scent of vanilla is also often recalled after an angel visitation. You may wish to burn vanilla oil or incense sticks when you meditate with your own angels
Violets	As with roses, this scent is often noted when angels appear in visitations, especially when associated with healing the sick, with births and crossings over to the other-side.
White Sage	Used for cleansing spaces to raise the energy vibration before magical work and angel contact (see also Frankincense)

Traditionally used as dried bundles of herb (smudge sticks), where the herb is lit, blown out, and the smoke is moved around the area to be cleansed. Traditionally the smoke would be distributed around the room with a feather, or you can use your hand or blow the smoke into the corners of the room

17

Angels and Astrology

Angels and Astrology

strology in its simplest form is the relationship of the stars in association with the zodiac. Years ago the phrase 'leader' or 'ruler of' would have been used rather than 'association', but the translation is much the same. Angels are also said to have control and rule over the stars, and the associations of each have been historically compared many times. Magical traditions in particular have combined the two. The word zodiac literally translates to 'the circle of animals'!

ANGELS OF THE ZODIAC

Humans were charting the passage of the stars as long as 30,000 years ago. Archaeologists have found bone fragments with star cycles on them. The Chaldeans (from Assyria) charted the stars as fixed in space but the planet (the Moon, Venus, Mercury, Mars, Jupiter and Saturn) as moving. They noted that the planets moved in front of these fixed star positions. Over time they became aware of when planets were in particular positions, and noted that similar events would occur. Mars seemed particularly visible when they were ready to go to war, for example – hence the association with Mars with conflict (Mars is the 'god' of war). Over longer periods of time, these associations became more detailed and specific, and so the signs of the zodiac were created.

The zodiac is split into 12 separate signs, associated with the known 12 star constellations. Traditionally, various gods have also been linked to the zodiac, which may be one explanation for the current link to angels and astrology. The relationships are one of similarities. Mars rules over (or is associated with) the sign of Aries for example; it is also connected to the month of March and ruled over by the angel Malahieael. But the angel Sammael is also said to rule over the planet Mars, which would then link Aries…to the angel Sammael! Phew! A little confusing!

There are many similarities between astrology and angelic tiers. In the Islamic texts, the four throne bearers of Allah are made up of the hierarchical levels of the Cherubim, Archangels and Angels and Guardian Angels. Each of the throne bearers was represented by different symbols (a human man, a bull, a lion and an eagle). These symbols are also used in the signs of the zodiac. A human figure (traditionally a male) is the image associated with Aquarius, Taurus is the bull, Leo the lion and the eagle was used in early astrology to represent the sign of Scorpio (which is now usually illustrated as a scorpion or snake).

Other associations come from long-held traditions, religions and magical works. It is not always possible to discover the original instigation. Texts connecting angels with astrology appear at different times, and even now you find new interpretations.

Zodiac Sign	Angels and Archangels
Aquarius	Cambiel (an angel of the 9th hour) and Gabriel (who appears in some places as the angel of January). Also associated with Archangel Uriel
Pisces	Barcheil (sometimes listed as one of the 7 archangels), the angel of February. Pisces is also associated with Archangel Gabriel
Aries	Malahidael (meaning 'fullness of God') or Machidiel (the angel of March). Also associated with Archangel Raphael
Taurus	Asmodel (the angel of April); also associated with Archangel Michael
Gemini	Ambriel (the angel of May); also associated with Archangel Uriel
Cancer	Muriel (the angel of June); also associated with Archangel Gabriel
Leo	Verchiel (the angel of July); also associated with Archangel Raphael
Virgo	Hamaliel (the angel of August); also associated with Archangel Michael
Libra	Zuriel (meaning 'my rock is God' and the angel of September) or Uriel. Also associated with Archangel Uriel.
Scorpio	Barbiel (the angel of October); also associated with Archangel Gabriel
Sagittarius	Advachiel or Adnachiel, (the angel of November); also associated with Archangel Raphael
Capricorn	Hanael (meaning 'Glory, or Grace of God', the angel of December); also associated with Archangel Michael

Working With Your Zodiac Angel

Call on your zodiac angel to help you with everyday problems. In time you will build up an association with this angel. Your astrological angel will work perfectly with the personality of your birth sign. Your association will bring you a type of kindred spirit and understanding. You'll have 'the perfect angel for the perfect job'. You can work with the angels above or with the angels whose personality traits are similar to those of your birth sign. For example, the planet Mercury is the planet of communication; Archangel Gabriel is the messenger (or communicating) angel … and so it goes round again.

BIRTH SIGN/ ZODIAC	RULING PLANET	ANGEL OVER THE RULING PLANET	BIRTH SIGN/ ZODIAC PERSONALITY TRAITS	ANGELS WITH ASSOCIATED ATTRIBUTES
Aquarius	Uranus	Planet not listed or known when ancient lists were created	Compassionate and independant	Chamuel and Zadkiel
Pisces	Neptune Saturn	Planet not listed or known when ancient lists were created	Receptive and subtle	Raphael and Raziel
Aries	Mars	Camael or Zamael or Sammael	Assertive and insistent	Abdiel and Uriel
Taurus	Venus	Aniel (Anael) or Haniel	Honourable and determined	Abdiel and Uriel
Gemini	Mercury	Michael or Mercury	Versatile and animated	Raguel and Gabriel
Cancer	Moon	Gabriel	Emotional and intuitive	Ariel and Haniel
Leo	Sun	Raphael and Michael	Powerful and dramatic	Haniel and Michael

Birth Sign/ Zodiac	Ruling Planet	Angel over the Ruling Planet	Birth Sign/ Zodiac Personality Traits	Angels with Associated Attributes
Virgo	Mercury	Michael or Raphael	Analytical and authoritative	Sariel and Michael
Libra	Venus	Aniel (Anael) or Sammael	Harmonius and diplomatic	Azrael and Jeremiel
Scorpio	Pluto	Not listed or known when ancient lists were created	Passionate and commanding	Michael and Uriel
Sagittarius	Jupiter	Zadkiel or Zachariel	Optimistic and independant	Jophiel and Ariel
Capricorn	Saturn	Kafziel, Zaphiel or Orifiel	Dutiful and disciplined	Metatron and Sandalphon

Connecting With Your Birth Sign Angel

Using the many ideas listed in the next chapter, Communicating With Your Angels, you can include your 'zodiac angel' name. One section suggests ways of contacting your angel by writing. If you are a Capricorn, you could write directly to your birth angels of Metatron and Sandalphon and ask them to help you with your challenge.

Other communication ideas include things such as angel altars, and you could include a representation of *your* angel as part of your display. You could ask your zodiac angel to communicate with you directly in dreams or to inspire you whilst you sleep, or call on your zodiac angel when you pray.

You can also ask your zodiac angel to come to you when you meditate. Angels are able to reach us and inspire us more easily when we are in deeply relaxed states. Occultists believe that our spiritual body lifts out of our physical body during dream states, and that also happens when in deep meditational states. Ask your zodiac angel to reach you and communicate with you at this time.

Angels can help to lead us to the right person or someone with the perfect skill or information to assist us in our task. Watch out for this person or perfect situation coming into your life. Know that the angels will be helping us to help ourselves. Do you need a person who is passionate and commanding? Maybe your angel will bring someone with the zodiac sign of Scorpio into your life. Do you need someone who is receptive and subtle? You could ask your angel to attract someone who has the attributes of a Pisces. Alternatively you can leave your zodiac angel to do what they do best of all and just get on with their job! Remember that all we have to do is ask them.

ANGELS OF THE PLANETS

Angels of the Moon

According to tradition, there are 28 angels that rule the 28 mansions of the moon. Occult (the word literally translates as 'the unknown') practices make use of these forces for magical use. You can combine them with angels of the hours, angels of the months and so on to prepare the most auspicious time for your communication work. The 28 angels are:

1 Geniel	8 Amnediel	15 Atliel	22 Geliel
2 Enediel	9 Barbiel	16 Azeruel	23 Requiel
3 Anixiel	10 Ardifiel	17 Adriel	24 Abrinael
4 Azariel	11 Neciel	18 Egibiel	25 Aziel
5 Gabriel	12 Abdizuel	19 Amutiel	26 Tagriel
6 Dirachiel	13 Jazeriel	20 Kyriel	27 Atheniel
7 Schliel	14 Ergediel	21 Bethnael	28 Amnixiel

Each phase of the moon has corresponding angelic forces. For the most powerful meditations and affirmations you can try calling on the angel of the hour, the angel of the week, the month and your own angel of the zodiac – all to work together!

Angels of the hours of the day

In traditional astrology, the time between sunrise and sunset was further separated into hours, each with a different ruling planet. The seven earliest discovered planets were the ones that were used at this time (this includes the Sun and the Moon). Uranus, Neptune and Pluto are not included.

Each of the angels and associated planets circle round and around – much like the planets themselves. So, Michael is followed by Gabriel, and then Samael, Raphael, Sachiel, Aniel and Cassiel, over and over in the same order. The association with planets to each angel remains the same. Michael is the angel associated with the Sun, Gabriel with the Moon, etc.

Angels of the Hours of the Night

Work with the angels of the hours at the correct time to create the most auspicious time for meditations and affirmations. The ancients would use this knowledge to make important decisions, carry out tasks and plan future events. As you would guess, there are parallels between the astrological associations of the planets and those of the angels!

Teamwork is a great idea – you can never get too much help, or too many angels!

ANGELS AND PLANETS

Hour of the Day	SUN	MON	TUES	WED	THUR	FRI	SAT
1	Michael Sun	Gabriel Moon	Samael Mars	Raphael Mercury	Sachiel Jupiter	Aniel Venus	Cassiel Saturn
2	Aniel Venus	Cassiel Saturn	Michael Sun	Gabriel Moon	Samael Mars	Raphael Mercury	Sachiel Saturn
3	Raphael Mercury	Sachiel Jupiter	Aniel Venus	Cassiel Saturn	Michael Sun	Gabriel Moon	Samael Mars
4	Gabriel Moon	Samael Mars	Raphael Mercury	Sachiel Jupiter	Aniel Venus	Cassiel Saturn	Michael Sun
5	Cassiel Saturn	Michael Sun	Gabriel Moon	Samael Mars	Raphael Mercury	Sachiel Saturn	Aniel Venus
6	Sachiel Saturn	Aniel Venus	Cassiel Saturn	Michael Sun	Gabriel Moon	Samael Mars	Raphael Mercury
7	Samael Mars	Raphael Mercury	Sachiel Jupiter	Aniel Venus	Cassiel Saturn	Michael Sun	Gabriel Moon
8	Michael Sun	Gabriel Moon	Samael Mars	Raphael Mercury	Sachiel Jupiter	Aniel Venus	Cassiel Saturn
9	Aniel Venus	Cassiel Saturn	Michael Sun	Gabriel Moon	Samael Mars	Raphael Mercury	Sachiel Saturn
10	Raphael Mercury	Sachiel Jupiter	Aniel Venus	Cassiel Saturn	Michael Sun	Gabriel Moon	Samael Mars
11	Gabriel Moon	Samael Mars	Raphael Mercury	Sachiel Jupiter	Aniel Venus	Cassiel Saturn	Michael Sun
12	Cassiel Saturn	Michael Sun	Gabriel Moon	Samael Mars	Raphael Mercury	Sachiel Saturn	Aniel Venus

ANGELS AND PLANETS

Hour of the Night	SUN	MON	TUES	WED	THUR	FRI	SAT
1	Sachiel Saturn	Aniel Venus	Cassiel Saturn	Michael Sun	Gabriel Moon	Samael Mars	Raphael Mercury
2	Samael Mars	Raphael Mercury	Sachiel Jupiter	Aniel Venus	Cassiel Saturn	Michael Sun	Gabriel Moon
3	Michael Sun	Gabriel Moon	Samael Mars	Raphael Mercury	Sachiel Jupiter	Aniel Venus	Cassiel Saturn
4	Aniel Venus	Cassiel Saturn	Michael Sun	Gabriel Moon	Samael Mars	Raphael Mercury	Sachiel Saturn
5	Raphael Mercury	Sachiel Jupiter	Aniel Venus	Cassiel Saturn	Michael Sun	Gabriel Moon	Samael Mars
6	Gabriel Moon	Samael Mars	Raphael Mercury	Sachiel Jupiter	Aniel Venus	Cassiel Saturn	Michael Sun
7	Cassiel Saturn	Michael Sun	Gabriel Moon	Samael Mars	Raphael Mercury	Sachiel Saturn	Aniel Venus
8	Sachiel Saturn	Aniel Venus	Cassiel Saturn	Michael Sun	Gabriel Moon	Samael Mars	Raphael Mercury
9	Samael Mars	Raphael Mercury	Sachiel Jupiter	Aniel Venus	Cassiel Saturn	Michael Sun	Gabriel Moon
10	Michael Sun	Gabriel Moon	Samael Mars	Raphael Mercury	Sachiel Jupiter	Aniel Venus	Cassiel Saturn
11	Aniel Venus	Cassiel Saturn	Michael Sun	Gabriel Moon	Samael Mars	Raphael Mercury	Sachiel Saturn
12	Raphael Mercury	Sachiel Jupiter	Aniel Venus	Cassiel Saturn	Michael Sun	Gabriel Moon	Samael Mars

18

Communicating With Your Angels

Communicating With Your Angels

Are you looking for ways of communicating with your angels? Here are a few ideas to help you.

Our angels are watching over us all the time, it is only that we are not aware of them. Communicating with your angels can be fun. Making contact with your angel can be a life-changing experience.

In modern times, angels want to make their presence known and invite communication with humankind. Each person must follow their own intuition and inner guidance as to how this communication might work for them. To show careful judgement with unseen guidance goes without saying.

Are you communicating with an angel? Check, check and check again. Does the energy feel right? Is the guidance relevant and favourable? Angel communication will be loving and non-judgemental. Angels do not tell us what to do but they may shine a light on suitable paths. The choice is always ours. We are always born with free will. Trust your own feelings and senses.

Before starting your angel communication, imagine the loving guidance of God. Remember that the angels are His own gift to the world, and all worlds. He sends his angels to help us. Breathe in the love of this universal energy, imagine it surrounding you and filling your inner being. Take time to relax and prepare for contact with your own angel guides. When you are ready to begin, look at some of the suggestions that follow.

Some of the things listed below will make you feel excited. Are you a creative person? Do you like to make things and work with your hands? Then follow the suggestions for crafting objects. Do you prefer something more physical? Then read the ideas relating to dance and see how that might work for you. Eventually you will come across your own ideas or the angels will inspire you. Write them in your angel journal!

ANGEL AFFIRMATIONS

What is an angel affirmation? Affirmations are a form of reinforcement of a 'positive thought'. We know that angels love to help us and only need our permission to do so. We can ask the angels to help us with our own goals and aid us in our motivation to make our wishes and dreams to come true.

It is useful to understand the role of our angels so that we know what they can and cannot do. An angel cannot live our life for us or take away our life challenges. What an angel can do is to help us to 'get through' life's problems by giving us the strength to do so, and by bringing useful people into our life. Think of your angels as working the way that a good friend might. A friend is a 'shoulder to cry on' when you fall out with your partner; someone who recommends a plumber when the kitchen sink springs a leak; someone who celebrates your successes and commiserates with you when things go wrong. Think of your angels as your very best friends.

What goals do you want to achieve? What plans do you have in your life? Let the angels help you. Do you need to loose weight? Do you want to make new friends? Would you like to study for a new career? The angels can help you with any of these things and many more. There is one 'rule' though: your affirmation has to be about you and how the angels can help *you* change your life.

It would be wrong to ask your angels to get your teenage son to help more around the house, or to make your neighbour suddenly find you more attractive. This is about your own 'free will' and not about manipulating anyone else's life to your ends. However, you could ask your angels to bring you ideas on how to improve your relationships with your son, or help you be more confident when talking with your neighbour.

Make sure your intent is clear and ethical

Then you need to decide exactly what you want from your future self; write it down in as much detail as you can:

'…I am fit and healthy. I am happy with my life path. My body is the perfect weight for my size and build. My skin is clear and fresh. I look after my body and ensure that I eat healthy and perfectly balanced food every day. I always take regular exercise so that I retain my body in its peak condition … My angels work with me to achieve my goals.'

Feel the goal happening, imagine it as if it had already happened to you, and always write in the here and now

Keep your statements positive. Say 'I am fit and healthy', rather than 'I wish I wasn't so fat!' Your higher self will hear you say 'fat' and will work with that! Not your intention at all.

Keep all statements positive

Organize your goal and wish-list into a series of little sentences. If you are creative, you could use phrases which will fit your favourite tune:

- ♥ 'I am always calm and at peace with the world. My angels are working alongside me.'

- ♥ 'I always reflect perfect confidence, knowing my angels are at my side in difficult situations.'

- ♥ 'My angels have assisted me in achieving my maths certificate.'

- ♥ 'I have a beautiful garden. My dream has been achieved with the help of my spiritual guardians.'

Or use short snappy statements:

- ♥ For the stressed – 'Calm inside equals calm outside.'

- ♥ For the shy – 'Confidence is as confidence does.'

- ♥ For the student – 'I am a grade A student.'

- ♥ For the gardener – 'Perfect plants will come to me!'

Or rhyming pairs:

- ♥ 'Peace reflects the inner me – I'm as calm, as calm can be…'

- ♥ 'The world will see my happy face – my mind is in a confident place…'

- ♥ 'Passing tests is easily done – my maths certificate is easily won…'

- ♥ 'The perfect garden comes my way – and beautiful plants will arrive today…'

OK, OK so I'm not a great poet! Sometimes if your poems are funny, it works even better! You are more likely to remember. Giggle whilst you work!

Use phrases and sayings that will help you remember your goals – not forgetting to ask your angels to help you

So how do you use these positive angel affirmations? Here are some suggestions:

- ♥ Write your affirmation down on a slip of paper – place it under your pillow and say it every morning and evening. Remember to thank your angels for their help, as if your goal had already been achieved.

- ♥ Type out your affirmation. Use attractive colours and fonts, and print it onto lightweight card or certificate paper. Frame and hang your affirmation in a prominent place where you will see it daily (over your desk, near to the kettle or hanging in the bathroom for example!).

- ♥ If you know how to do calligraphy (beautiful, traditional handwriting) then write your sayings and frame them. Maybe now is a good time to learn?

♥ Write your slogans into your diary or journal so that you reflect on them regularly.

♥ Years ago, women would embroider sayings onto pillows, tablecloths and bedding. Many households had framed 'cross-stitch' pictures on the wall with the family motto happily surrounded by flowers or other decoration. Sayings such as 'Bless this House' were popular, but you must create your own version, obviously.

♥ How about having it engraved onto something, or, if your affirmations are long ones, perhaps just the initials of your affirmation added to the inside of a ring. 'AAA' might mean 'Angels Always Around' to you, or perhaps 'HAH' could be your way of remembering you are 'Healthy and Happy'. Again, remember that humour helps!

♥ My local stationers sell 'self-laminating cards' the size of a credit card or room pass key. Your affirmations can be reproduced onto a card and then covered or protected with plastic. Your card will be the perfect size to carry around in a wallet or pop into the back pocket of your jeans.

♥ Rather than make your own angelic affirmations you might find something suitable that you could use at home. Fridge magnets are a useful source of fun and positive sayings. Check out your local card shop or search the Internet for something you can frame which inspires your goals. Keyrings, too, can be useful. My husband carries his car keys on a keychain which reminds him to 'Never drive faster than your angels can fly.'

♥ When your sayings and affirmations no longer have the same impact, or you stop noticing them, look at ways of rephrasing them so that the ideas remain fresh in your mind. Keep your goals alive and always moving forward.

Remember that *you* are the driver of the bus that carries you and your needs, aspirations, hopes, fears and achievements. Your angels are the bus conductors who are there to help get you to the right destination. Take a step down that road, and your angels are right there beside you, holding your hand. Angels won't live your life, but they will help you to live it yourself! Take control, take charge and make things happen for *you*. You are the writer of your own story and your angels are the crowd, cheering *you* on!

ANGEL ALTARS

Angel altars work in much the same way that any altar might, and are easily assembled: gather together a collection of items with special significance to you, and place them within an altar space. Ideas for an altar space include:

♥ A corner of your garden, maybe under a tree, or a private space under an archway or slightly hidden from the house.

♥ A shelf in your bedroom.

♥ A small coffee table.

♥ A mantelpiece over a fireplace.

♥ The top of a chest of drawers.

If you really don't have space for a permanent angel altar you can collect your special items together in a pretty box and arrange them on a tray (or on the top of the box) when you are ready to meditate or want to talk to the angels.

An angel altar can include many things and is only limited by your imagination. You might want to use some or all of the following:

♥ A representative or two of what an angel is to you. This might be an angel figurine, an angel pin, an angel coin or token, a postcard or a picture of an angel. You could use several if you have them.

♥ A candle, traditionally used to bring in the light. You could choose candles scented with natural aromatherapy oils or pick candles with colours associated with the energy of a specific archangel (see page 257).

♥ Angel cards in an open bowl so that you can easily pick one or two each day.

♥ A crystal or a stone which appeals to you (for more on angels and crystals, see page 262).

- ♥ White feathers (an angel 'symbol') – perhaps some that you have found yourself.

- ♥ Scented oils or natural herbs.

- ♥ Incense sticks.

- ♥ Fresh flowers or a flowering pot plant (angels are said to appear on the scent of flowers).

- ♥ Your angel journal or notebook containing your positive affirmations or healing experiences.

- ♥ Pretty photograph frames with pictures of your loved ones or images of people to whom you wish the angels send help and healing.

- ♥ Angel books.

- ♥ Scented sachets or packets.

- ♥ Rose petals or flower heads floating in a glass or attractive china bowl of water.

- ♥ Angel sprinkles or 'confetti', as it is often called.

- ♥ Items decorated with butterflies (as a representation of spirit).

- ♥ Small trinket boxes – maybe those decorated with angel or cherubs.

- ♥ A small photo clip – useful for displaying inspirational messages.

Your angel altar can be displayed on a silk scarf (I have one with gold angels printed on!) or an old-fashioned lace table or tray cloth – or anything else which inspires you. Remember that there are no rules here. If you feel inspired and uplifted by your display then it is right for you! It is important, however, to keep your flowers fresh and your area 'dust free' by dusting or changing it around regularly. An angel altar is a point of focus for your angel prayers and meditations. Given time this space will gather energy of its own. Prayers and positive affirmations will form a blanket of loving power within this space and you will feel uplifted just by walking into this area. The altar is not for the worship of angels but for you to create your own point of energy or prayer or meditation for your own insights and ideas.

ANGELIC ARTWORK

People with no previous ability to draw seem to be able to draw angels. The angels appear to 'channel' the images through the human instrument (our bodies), producing beautiful portraits of the angels themselves. Angels have many different looks – over the years the way angels are portrayed in artworks has changed, sometimes dramatically! What does an angel look like to you?

If you want to have a go at this you need no particular skill, just some suitable equipment: paper, pens and inks, paints and paintbrushes, pencils, crayons, chalks – whatever inspires you.

To gather inspiration, you may want to start with a prayer. You could write down your request to the angels, to help you. Play some inspirational or relaxing music, or light a candle (stand it on a table away from your paper for safety).

Become totally relaxed and just 'go with the flow'. Don't worry too much about what you actually produce on the paper. Do not judge the final result. When you have finished, tidy away your work and put it all together in a safe place until you feel inspired to try again.

Over time, your angels will learn how to work with you, and you with them. Images may appear to 'improve' to your own artistic eye. There is no right or wrong technique, just *your* way.

Enjoy the experience.

ANGEL ATMOSPHERE

What is an angel atmosphere? I sometimes hold angel workshops and one of the most important things is to create an angel atmosphere – to lift the energy of the room to one where the angels can come closely into our own energy field.

Angels are often associated with the strong smell of flowers, particularly roses, gardenias and lilacs. Burning high-quality incense which uses the natural essence of these flowers, I believe, helps to create a higher vibrational energy within the room. For communication with the angels, use natural frankincense aromatherapy oil (three drops in water, on the top of an oil burner – follow the manufacturer's instructions if available).

Rooms for angel work should always be cleansed – and literally cleaned – before you begin. You wouldn't invite visitors into your personal space without dusting and vacuuming first would you? Make sure everything in the room sparkles – windows (a reflection of your 'view of the world'), fabrics and furnishings, rugs and floorings and any decoration. Clean and fresh.

Next you can energize the space. Use a drum (if you are lucky enough to own one) and bang it in rhythm, particularly into the corners and hard-to-reach spaces. Stir up that still energy! If you don't have a drum, you can clap into the corners or even ring a bell.

I like to take a natural incense stick and move the smoke around the room – all the while asking for the loving energy of the angels to come into the space. I do not 'invoke' the angels; I invite them.

Next, I play relaxing music. There are several beautiful CDs that have been created especially to work with angels as 'angel music' (an Internet search would probably bring up several companies that do these). Sometimes, I even dance around the room (but don't tell anyone!).

I always dedicate a white candle to the angels. Those little tea-lights, or 'night-lights' as we called them when I was a little girl, are perfect.

Then you are ready to begin. Always thank the angels for their presence, and remember to blow out your candle afterwards.

ANGELS IN THE BATH!

Yes really! In spiritual terms, bathing is a very cleansing and uplifting experience. Angels can communicate more easily with us when we are in a relaxed state, so talking to the angels whilst you bathe actually makes a lot of sense.

- ❤ Fill the bathroom with scented candles and dim the lights – create the atmosphere for an 'angel-chat'.

- ❤ Run a warm bath and add a few drops of your favourite essential oil. Rose is perfect. The pure and traditional scent uplifts the mood. Any strong scented flower oil or vanilla (another angel favourite) would be fine.

- ❤ Drop a few rose petals in the bath (pop them in a muslin bag or tack two cotton hankies together, if you don't want a mushy mess!).

- ❤ Spoil yourself with fluffy towels and a beautiful bathrobe – lift your spirits.

Relax in the warm water and talk to your angel friends – just *know* that they are there and can hear you. Remember that their words are kind and loving. Expect your answers as positive thoughts or feelings, ideas or inspiration.

Rozalynd wrote to kindly share her own 'bath story', while at the same time telling me '…I have never written a letter like this before.' People always feel a little embarrassed at sharing these stories, but this little story is typical of the ones I receive on angel experiences while people are bathing! So it doesn't seem so strange to me.

'I was reading an article in a magazine about Angels, and how to communicate with them. The article said to find a quiet place where you won't be disturbed. As I have six children the only place I get "undisturbed" is in the bath!

I lit a white candle, closed my eyes for a while, and then I felt like I was floating, dreaming, just like the feeling you get under anaesthetic before you go completely under. I can't put it into words properly, but it felt so peaceful. My head went back and to the side, as if resting on a shoulder, and I wanted to stay there.

I remember asking, "If you're really there please show me a sign." My son called me at that moment, so I opened my eyes and reached for the candle to blow it out. Some of the wax dropped accidentally into the bath and the wax made the shape of a perfect, white, fluffy set of angel's wings!

Placing the candle back in the holder, I stepped out of the bath, and leant over the bath to cup the wax into my hands and carefully lift it out. After I was dressed I lit the candle again. This time I deliberately dropped wax into the bath water, but however often I did it I never managed to repeat the same pattern.

Nothing like this has ever happened to me before, but I hope it will happen again, the feeling was one of such peace.'

ANGEL CALLING CARDS

Calling cards? Now that's a lovely old-fashioned idea. Ladies would call at a friend's (often spontaneously) and if they were not 'at home' (which sometimes just meant they were not receiving visitors that day, even if they were in the house), the caller would leave their card (by passing it to the maid or butler to leave on a silver tray, or just by posting it through the door).

What fun to leave your calling card! Using your angel symbol (draw something of your own) and your name (and maybe a phone number if you wish), carry your angel calling cards around in a purse or pocket. When calling on friends, especially if they have been unwell or particularly wanted to see you, you can leave your card if they are out. What a great way to let people know you cared enough to call. Let the angels help you communicate your message of caring – you could even add a little note on the back:

'Sorry you were out when I called. Hope you are feeling better…'

ANGEL CIRCLES

Do you have friends who are interested in angels? Why not create your own group or 'circle' to study and work with angels?

- ♥ Take it in turns to have get-togethers at each other's houses – make your meetings on the same date or day every month or week so that people remember.

- ♥ Each member could bring a small token gift to the person hosting the circle.

- ♥ Swap angel stories with each other. Do you have miracle stories of healing or love in your family? Angel stories are meant for sharing – spread the joy.

- ♥ Angel books are very uplifting. How about creating a 'swap library' of any you may have finished with. Perhaps a small donation to charity could be made to borrow a book? Place one person in charge of tracking books and making sure they are returned safely!

- ♥ Pick out angel divination cards and do readings for yourselves and others in the group.

- ♥ Take the opportunity to play angel CDs and review each other's collections of celestial sounds.

- ♥ Play guided angel meditation CDs and all meditate together. Swap notes afterwards.

- ♥ Try some of the ideas in this chapter – writing with your angels or perhaps making collages.

- ♥ Work on your angel journals together.

- ♥ Work as a group to ask the angels for healing for those in need. Bring newspaper cuttings on world situations and troubled spots, and photographs of family and friends in need of healing. One person could be placed in charge of keeping a healing book. Pray to the angels together to assist those in need.

♥ Share ideas of more ways in which you can connect with your own angels.

You do not have to live close together to form an angel circle, if this is a problem. Internet groups work very well and there will never be any lack of support.

ANGEL COLLAGE

A collage is the ultimate in re-cycling. Starting with a large piece of card or stiff paper, you collect together pretty scraps and stick them together to create one new image. You can frame it afterwards. I have done this several times to create a positive vision of things I wanted in my life – it works every time! Try it and see if it can work for you.

Ideas for items to add to your angel collage:

♥ Pictures of angels cut from wrapping paper.

♥ Stickers illustrated with angels, flowers, fairies and butterflies.

♥ Dried, pressed flowers and leaves.

♥ Christmas and birthday cards are a great source of images.

♥ Scan images from books and other suitable pictures (check they are copyright free).

♥ Photographs of a loved one – or loved ones on the 'other-side'.

♥ Angel glitter.

♥ Images from the Internet.

- ❤ Inspirational poems and angel sayings. You can type these up or write them out using gold and silver pens.

- ❤ Pictures of pets.

- ❤ How about including lists of 'wish' words – things or qualities that you would like in your life.

- ❤ You could stick on images which represent your dreams and hopes for the future.

- ❤ You can write your name using stick-on or rub-down letters, or print words and phrases using a computer with a script lettering (or trace the letters below). This font is called Zapf Chancery.

A B C D E F G H I J K
L M N O P Q R S T U
V W X Y Z

Most important of all – Have Fun!

ANGEL COOKING

I realize that angels don't actually eat, but we do! Communicating with your angels is about feeling good inside and nothing makes you feel better than good cooking. My daughter always makes those 'fairy cakes' (tiny cupcakes in paper cases), and you may find a recipe for 'angel cake'. Cake is nice and comforting to many people. I prefer something which is a little less fattening but if you've ever heard the saying 'a little of what you fancy does you good', then you'll know exactly what I mean.

If salad is sumptuous for you, then make that. If bread is bliss for you, bake bread, and if pasta is perfect for your pleasure, prepare that. Create a meal for fun and, even better, lay the table for two people. It could be just you and a friend, or you and your angel. Create some 'food for thought'. 'Take care of your body' and other similar messages appear on many angel divination cards.

Cooking (and maybe more often, 'baking') gives you the opportunity to 'be an angel'. Making a fruit cake? Bake one for your elderly neighbour who lives on her own. Creating a casserole for one? Double up the portions and take it round to your friend who has just given birth, or maybe recently come out of hospital. Spread love and friendship – it's contagious. Sharing food that you have created yourself is like sharing your energy with others, and passing on a little practical love. Prepare a meal for someone you love today and ask the angels to bless the meal for you. Go on, be an angel.

ANGEL DANCING AND MUSIC

OK, so I know you can't actually 'see' your angels, and I can imagine it might not be easy to join them in the last waltz, but let me explain further…

People in ancient cultures would regularly dance themselves into trance states to enable them to talk to the spirit realms. Whirling and twirling, round and round, following the beat … how easy it is to 'loose yourself' in the music … to get carried away by the rhythm?

Dancing is like continuous exercise in which a person can get 'high'. You can feel an adrenaline rush! This is the understanding behind dancing with your angels, but I'm not asking you to do this. Dancing is a way of both releasing and reaching emotions. Dancing is something that people do when they are in love. Dancing is something that small children do spontaneously in fun, and what teenagers do for energy release.

Dancing, more than any other way, can relax the body so that the angels can communicate with you. You are not so much 'dancing with angels', as they are dancing with *you*.

OK, so what are the techniques? Dancing is best when it is done instinctively. You do not have to please anyone but yourself. Dance alone or with friends. Technique is unimportant. The dancing is about how it makes you 'feel'.

Setting the scene:

♥ If you are inside you may prefer to lock the door so you won't be disturbed.

♥ Take the phone off the hook and switch off your mobile.

♥ You will be more comfortable if it is at least half an hour after you have eaten and not so long after you have eaten that you will be distracted by feeling hungry.

♥ Dance barefoot if the flooring is comfortable. Otherwise, wear something simple and lightweight like ballet pumps.

♥ Turn up the heating or turn it down (bearing in mind that dancing can make you hot), so that your body is at a comfortable temperature.

♥ Have a drink of water nearby so that you can refresh yourself without having to break your movements.

♥ Choose your music in advance by selecting tracks that suit your mood. Classical or 'angel music' both work well. You may prefer something slower or something with a beat. Have a selection ready so that you can change the mood as you go.

♥ Consider using an instrument while you dance – a drum, or something to shake out a rhythm. (An old tin or jar filled with dried peas or rice works well.)

Here are a few things to try.

Receiving love: Dress in simple clothing which will not restrict your movement in any way, then close the curtains. Lock the door if it will make you feel less inhibited and, when you are ready, sway gently to the rhythm. Do not feel embarrassed as no one can see you. Rock gently from side to side. Imagine you are being cradled in your angel's wings. Try to continue for at least a whole track to gain the full benefit of this movement.

Creating positive change: Dress in clothing which reflects the person you want to be. Would you like your angels to help you to bring more humour into your life? Then wear clown make-up! Want to appear more mysterious? Wear dark glasses! Have fun with this, and come up with some of your own suggestions.

Look for items that will indicate your chosen change. Dance with pictures cut from magazines, or wear a pin or brooch with positive sayings and affirmations (write them on to cardboard and tape a safety pin on the back). Play music with an up-beat rhythm. Say or sing your message while you dance like crazy! Play music with appropriate lyrics – 'I want to be free', or 'I'm going to wash that man right out of my hair'! Or select a song with the word 'angel' in the lyrics (there are hundreds of these). Sing very loudly – especially useful to remove aggression!

Protection and energizing: Play a series of songs where the beat gets progressively faster. Or one track where the song gets faster towards the end (Ravel's *Bolero* is a good example and was once used by the ice-skating champions Torvel and Dean in their Olympic performance).

As you reach the faster speeds, ask for your angels to come close to you – feel this happening. To start with it will feel like butterflies fluttering as the sense will be gentle. As your heart begins to beat faster you will notice a change in your energy field. Lift your heart and let in this positive energy. Imagine your body filling with and surrounded by positive white light. Build this energy in your mind. Imagine this light as a protection from the angels. Remember that 'imagination' is a powerful force and that all creation starts as an 'idea' before it becomes lodged in 'our reality'. Something moves from the 'astral realms of thought' into our earth plane or 'material plane'.

When you are ready, start to slow your movements down. Take your time, and slow down your heart rate a little at a time.

Create some movements and a dance of your own. Just consider a few safety tips. Dancing is a type of exercise. With all forms of exercise, make sure that you check with your doctor first – particularly if you plan to get energetic and you don't normally. Make sure you do not flail your arms around where you might knock or break something (be it an ornament or your arm!), and don't spin round so fast that you make yourself dizzy and crash into something (not in the house anyway). Some movements are better outside on safe, bouncy grass!

Dancing is fun with friends – choose a large open space or work in a large hall. If you're switching the phone off for a few hours, then do let someone know. You don't want to start an international panic because you suddenly become unavailable for any length of time.

Oh, and did I say 'have fun?' Those all-important words again.

Sometimes angels want to play music back. Kimber from the United States writes that she has welcomed angels into her life and they have lots of fun ways of making their presence known.

Once, Kimber was watching a television show with a woman who was talking about angels. Suddenly, her stereo popped on by itself. Kimber knew it was her own angel saying hello.

She began to talk to her angels, and would feel what she calls 'prickles', which let her know they were around her. Sometimes she'll feel the prickles on her arm or on the top of her head. But it always gets her attention.

Kimber has a music box on her desk that plays when you wind it up and then open the top. She hadn't wound it or played it for months and months. One day, she walked into her room and heard the music box playing. It stopped after a few notes. She sat down at her computer, and after about ten minutes she asked if anyone was there. The music box played a few more notes, and Kimber said, 'Hello! Thanks!'

She also thinks her angels sound the windchimes in her kitchen. They tinkle even without a breeze. Kimber feels the more she opens up to her angels, the more they present themselves to her.

ANGEL DIVINATION CARDS

Anyone can read angel divination cards and you don't have to be psychic to do so. Angel divination cards are kind of oracles in the form of loving words, phrases or sentences laid out on individual cards (like playing cards), which you can dip into for inspirational and comforting messages.

We all have the ability to understand what these messages mean *to us*, and the same card pulled out several days in a row would probably mean different things each time – even when chosen by the same person.

Let's use an example. A card with a plant illustration and the word 'FLOWERS' printed on the front … what might that mean? The first day you choose the card, you might immediately think, 'I must spend some time tidying up the garden and making it look pretty for the spring.' The same card, the following day might bring to mind something entirely different: 'Perhaps I'll go and buy a plant for Aunty Marge who is in hospital.'

Divination cards, with their simple messages, enable us to tap into our 'inner knowing' or 'our inner guidance' – your angel helpers! There are many beautiful angel divination cards on the market or you can easily make your own.

Making Your Own Angel Divination Cards

Start with some thin card. You can use old Christmas or birthday cards (using the images of angels on the back!). An old credit card makes a good template. Then just hand-write your words or phrases on the back. Stationers sell lovely gold and silver pens which are perfect for this!

If you have access to a computer, you can use light card or a 'business card' template and type up your words in a nice italic or scroll-type lettering with a printed illustration on the reverse.

Alternatively you can use Christmas wrapping paper or angel stickers to decorate your cards. There is something very special about making your own angel divination cards. It gives you the opportunity to use words that have important meanings for *you*. You'll need around 36–44 cards to have a regular turnover of messages.

Here are some of my own inspirational phrases to start you off:

Security and Safety	*Creating Space*
Friends and Family	*Making Changes*
Faithful Pets	*A New Beginning*
Commune with Nature	*Bright Ideas*
Practical Assistance	*Spiritual Cleansing*
Support and Guidance	*Loving Light*
Wisdom and Knowledge	*Taking Control*
Bodily Care	*New Experience*
Wishes and Dreams	*Growth and Maturity*
Magic and Manifestations	*Caring and Sharing*
Divine Intervention	*Personal Peace*
Many Blessings	*Creative Ambitions*
Parties and Celebrations	*Innocent Children*
Fun and Games	*Following your Truth*

Welcome Relationships
Organization and Design
Awareness and Appreciation
Strength and Stamina

Each Uniquely Perfect
Natural Wonders
Holding Hands
Inner Guidance

How to Use Angel Divination Cards

Many angel divination cards come with an instruction book. Forget the book of instructions! (Well go on, read it if you must!) You don't need instructions, because there is no right or wrong way to use divination cards. Just follow your instincts. Here are a few ideas to inspire you.

- ♥ Pick one card a day. Prop it up where you will see it regularly. I like to use those clips for holding a single photograph, and stand it by my computer.

- ♥ Choose three cards together and 'read' all the phrases as a single message for yourself.

- ♥ Pick a card each time you have a question or need inspiration.

- ♥ Keep them in a pretty open dish or bowl and hand them around when friends pop over – it's a great conversation starter!

- ♥ Use your cards to do a Past, Present and Future reading. Lay out your cards in a simple 'spread'. Lay out three cards. Place the first card furthest away from you (this card indicates your past). Place the second card just in front of that (this card indicates your present situation). Lay the third card at the front (this card indicates your future).

Remember that all angel divination cards contain loving and positive messages. If you read something negative, look to your own self! Our angels do not judge us in any way whatsoever! It is simply not within their ability or role.

I received a letter from Charlotte about her own angel divination cards. She felt that they had helped her a lot.

She told me that for a long time she had felt 'different and gifted', and felt inspired to go to a healing mass. She said that the experience was fantastic and she felt like she should ask to be able to heal and help people.

Charlotte explained how she felt that she was blessed and found herself surrounded by a blinding white light, and felt great love. Shortly afterwards, she found some angel divination cards for sale in a magazine and sent off for them. Charlotte felt that she had found the tool she had been looking for.

She told me, 'My life is not the same. I read the cards for friends and I am amazed by what comes from my mouth and feelings that I see or pick up. I have been told that I am surrounded by angels.'

Charlotte feels the loving messages are coming from the angels themselves.

Angel divination cards are not a miracle communication tool, but I do feel that they are a gentle and loving way for us to pick up on loving contact and messages. We all have some natural, psychic ability and sometimes with a tool such as this, we feel confident in 'reading the message', which we could possibly have picked up anyway … if only we had the confidence to say what we feel!

Remember that each card can be read in many different ways, so you naturally use your own intuition to read the card anyway. You will get more confident with practice.

Give them a go and see if they will work for you.

ANGEL GARDENS AND OUTDOOR SPACES

Angels love to work with us in outdoor places. They find it easy to reach us when we are 'at one' with nature. This can be in a garden, a park, or perhaps somewhere in the mountains or by a lake.

Working with Water

Imagine walking along miles of beach … There is a long stretch of sand in Cornwall, England called Gwithian beach. As I step down onto the beach it is like finding the angels already waiting for me. The feeling you can create after many hours of deep meditation, an inner peace? I always find it here. Listening to the sound of the sea moving in and out; listening to the seagulls overhead and the soft whisper of the breeze. This is what I find when I am beside the sea – and particularly at Gwithian.

We found another place with a similar 'feel' about it when we went to the island of Fuerteventura. This island is part of the Canaries in the Atlantic off the west coast of Africa. Much of the island is old volcanic rocks and mountains, but hidden in little coves are beautiful beaches. The island is famous for them. On a family holiday we came across the most amazing place here too … and it was a lot warmer than Gwithian beach as well! You will find your own beaches, because for everyone these places must be of our own making.

You can recreate the sound of the sea with a tape recording. Make your own, or you can actually buy CDs with sea sounds on them. I have one at home. Sitting in a warm room with my eyes closed and the sound of the 'sea' playing in the background helps to take me to my relaxing 'angel beaches'.

I feel that the angels can reach us in places where we find our own perfect peace … a place where we reach our own inner meditation. For you this might be on a beach but it could just as easily be by a lake – or even on a lake. Water seems to help with the transferring of information. (Think of those inspirational thoughts that occur when we are in the bath!)

Do you find 'yourself' when you sit on the banks of a river? Do you love to watch the ducks go by, or are you one of the many fishermen (and woman) who 'fish' purely for the peace and not for the catch of the day! Some of them confess that they don't mind if they catch anything or not … but don't say I gave away their secret!

Parks and Gardens

Do you own a dog? Are you one of the many people who feel a walk doesn't seem right without a dog? Dogs are full of joy, and love nothing better than to run around in big open spaces. They love exploring and sniffing out new smells. Some of that joy and adventure can rub off on us. Who wants to go out in the rain and cold? Your dog does! And once we've braved the weather, don't we always feel better afterwards?

Take a toddler to the park and you see everything through their eyes. Every pretty stone is a magical tool, every daisy a work of art, every feather an angel's wing. Perhaps it is. Children see everything as an adventure. When I was a little girl I would love to go on a 'nature walk'. That inevitably meant taking a carrier bag or a basket (which is more 'romantic') and collecting things to take home. Acorns, conkers and fir cones came top of the list. Pretty stones with holes in them (in some cultures these holes are believed to be gateways to other worlds), or pebbles with 'sparkly bits' came a very close second.

We loved to search out branches with berries on and wild mushrooms growing under trees. Having scant knowledge of which of these were poisonous and which were safe we just looked at everything and picked none! Lovely gnarled old trees were magical too. Could there be whole communities of nature spirits, gnomes and fairies living in the branches? If there are fairies, then there must be angels too!

'Always leave room in your garden for the Angels to dance.'

ANON

The magic of these places can be recreated at home. You do not have to own a garden – a window box or a plant pot will do. Just work on a smaller scale. Groups of pot plants surrounding the chair you use for meditation and contemplation are a pleasure. Gather your own 'nature table', or place your angel figurines in your plant pots! No room for something like that? How about pots of home-grown herbs on your kitchen window sill? Bring yourself closer to nature and bring the angels closer to you.

ANGEL GIFTS

Have you ever noticed how many beautiful angel gifts are available in the shops and on the Internet? Angel products seem to be appropriate on any occasion. The little angel pins can be worn on a jacket collar or on the lapel of your coat. They are very small and distinct. I like to think they invite the angels to help and protect us.

I know many people who carry around those little angel coins and tokens. They are small enough to carry around in your pocket or wallet, or to put in the coin tray in your car.

Angel gifts are especially nice around religious holidays, and particularly appropriate for people in hospital. It brings a gentle reminder that the angels are close, and thinking about angels brings them closer still.

I have angels all around my working space. My own preference is for the little gold or white cherubs. I have them on cushions, pictures, frames and photo clips; I have them sitting on shelves and the top of cupboards and they even decorate candles and candlesticks. Don't worry – they are very discrete – most people do not notice them straight away!

I have a beautiful stained glass angel hanging in the window in front of my desk and a crystal etched with an angel also hangs in the window in front of me. Angels decorate notebooks and photograph albums and bookends! I like angels a lot. Even though I know that angels probably don't look the way that we portray them, it doesn't matter to the angels one bit.

Lots of companies send me angel products to review (lucky me!). A lovely gift box with glass angels arrived one day with a message from the manufacturer. These boxes of angels were 'winging' their way to the bedsides of people who were sick and in hospital – a lovely idea I thought!

The angel sprinkles or 'foil confetti' is lovely to pop into greetings cards and parcels. I even add them to my invoice envelopes! They do have a tendency to 'spill out' of your package! People have told me that they carry these little angels around in their purses. They are charming when added to cards for any celebration and anniversary – and adorable tucked into a greeting for a new-born baby. They are also perfect for sad occasions too, and make a nice comforting surprise for someone in grief – just pop a few inside a personal letter.

Angel stickers and papers are more readily available at Christmas – I like to buy items in the sales and keep them to use all year round.

People see angels in different ways, so always choose what feels right for you – or make things of your own. You will have the added advantage that your own creative energy is mixed with that of the angels. A gift of an angel symbol is a special gift indeed.

ANGELS AND HOUSEHOLD CHORES

We often daydream when we clean the house or wash the car. Repetitive and often-repeated chores lead our mind to stroll to more interesting subjects. With our minds in this relaxed and open place we raise ourselves spiritually to a state between waking and sleeping. Communication with our unseen spiritual helpers is just a thought away.

Angels place ideas into our minds rather than words (although you may hear words occasionally too). Having a two-way conversation is easy and the trick is to keep on working! The more boring the task, the easier it is for the mind to drift away. Just ask a question in your head. The answer will come. The answer is not always what you expect, but give some thought to the suggestions. Take the opportunity to look at the problem from a different perspective, a different point of view.

An angel's role is not to tell us what to do or solve every problem. Part of our task here on Earth is to learn and grow from our experiences, even (especially?) from our mistakes. Doing things wrong is often the best way to learn to do it right, or the right way for us. However, angels are perfectly placed to give us a clue. Their guidance is always sent with the intent of assisting our highest spiritual wellbeing.

Oh – and if your biggest worry is finding someone to help with the housework, then they can help with that too. Just ask. You might be surprised.

ANGEL JOURNAL

An angel journal is a private and personal record of your own. You can use it for many things:

- ♥ To keep a daily record of all the positive things that have happened each day in your life, like the gift of a compliment, seeing old friends, watching the birds visit your garden bird table, or the giggling of a child.

- ♥ To record the paranormal or magical things which have happened to you, your family and your friends.

- ♥ To record loving message, sayings, phrases or poems which inspire you.

- ♥ To stick letters, notes and cards received from friends and lovers.

- ♥ To list your hopes, dreams and desires.

- ♥ To keep cuttings from magazines and newspapers which have made you feel good.

- ♥ To record your angel information.

- ♥ To record your dreams and visions.

Not everyone has time to write in a journal every day but try and find time to fill in your journal several times a week if you can, or perhaps just put aside one special time every week for you and your angel journal.

Treat this as a sacred time for your creation.

- ♥ Make or buy something especially for the purpose of keeping your angel journal. Buy a pretty hard-backed notebook, or you could create your angel journal in a sparkly ring binder. Some people write their angel journal using a computer.

- ❤ Illustrate the pages as you feel inspired with drawings, sketches, stickers or cuttings.

- ❤ Choose a special pen especially for your journal.

- ❤ Find a private and safe place to keep your records. You could wrap it the traditional way using a piece of silk or velvet – and tie it closed with a length of ribbon or soft cord. If you enjoy sewing you could make and decorate a drawstring bag or place it in a special box. Perhaps the best place for you is in your bedroom in a drawer or cupboard.

- ❤ As with other angel rituals, you can light a candle and dedicate the book with a prayer.

- ❤ Sometimes the magic and miracles which happen in real life tend to get forgotten. By using this opportunity to record these special times, we are keeping the memories alive. There is a belief that if you acknowledge the enchantment in your everyday world you encourage more such experiences. I firmly believe this is true. Remember to record the magic in your life.

ANGEL LETTERS

Did you know you can write to your angels? You can use a notebook to record your letters but you can also write individual letters and place them under your pillow. Save them as you would special love letters and tie them together with pretty ribbon.

As with your angel journal you can set aside a special and private time to write your angels a letter. Do not expect the angels to pick up a pen and move it spookily through the air to reply, though, it doesn't quite work that way! You don't suddenly get taken over by a spirit! But you will feel their love.

If you are unsure that this will happen for you, write down your questions and answers as if it were actually working. Add your replies in such a way that 'if your angels were writing to you, what might they say?' Soon, the answers become automatic for you. You'll just know what to write, because you'll tune into their vibration. Never worry that you are making things up. Our creative imagination is the way we reach these inner worlds.

> *'Without this playing with fantasy no creative work has ever*
> *yet come to birth. The debt we owe to the play of the*
> *imagination is incalculable.'*
>
> C.G. JUNG

Before you begin, prepare as you would for other communications. Light a special candle and say a prayer.

Write your letter as you would to any special friend. Angels like beautiful words, but do not worry about spelling – it is of little importance. Begin with a special salutation:

'My Dearest angel of God...
How I wish to write with you on this special day, and I look forward to receiving any individual messages you may have for me in return. I bless your loving wisdom and would love to share some personal experiences with you and ask that you bring me words of comfort and joy...'

You may choose to start off in a similar way to the note above. You can ask your angel as many questions as you wish.

'I have been struggling with my work and wondered if you were around me during this time? I often feel alone and would like to invite you to draw close to me...'

Then continue with the pen as if you were aware of the thoughts and feelings your angels are sending you in return. Write down what you feel.

You may not hear words but usually pick up feelings from your angels. Just write what you feel in reply.

'

'My Beloved child

We, your angels, are with you always at your side, bringing you guidance and our whispered words of love. Know that we support you always in your hopes and dreams and are here for you always...'

Don't worry about doing it wrong. No one is going to see this. You are just practising, and may be surprised at the results you receive! Don't stop too long or deliberate over your words – just write, remembering that the angels' messages are always supportive and kind.

When you feel your questions have come to an end, remember to thank your angels for their support. You may say a prayer to close your communication session if you wish. Then blow out your candle at the end. Date your letter and put it away somewhere safe.

'Thank you, angels, for your loving words...'

Read it in a couple of days' time. You may be surprised at what you see.

Practice makes perfect and many people communicate with their angels in this way. Each message should become stronger and clearer.

ANGEL MAGIC IN DREAMS

Angels 'are' magic! Magic, in that 'the rules that govern our world, do not relate to the angels'. Their rules defy our natural laws but, of course, they are natural rules for the angels! Their world in the angelic realms is more fluid than that of our earthly plane. We see things as solid. However the objects and living beings in our world only 'seem' solid! In reality, they are not solid at all, but are made up of a moving mass of atoms and molecules.

By working with angels in our dreams we can move around more easily in this fluid world. Our angels can reach down into a middle space – we may not always remember however! Before drifting off to sleep, ask your angels for help. Take this time to communicate with your angels and guides and ask that they work with you in these magical realms.

I've had amazing inspiration and assistance whilst 'asleep'! I've woken up with the answer to problems, and the angels have even given me the name for a book I am working on! Tchaikovsky was a famous dreamer. He often woke with an idea for a composition. Many modern-day composers, such as Billy Joel, Paul McCartney and Sting, amongst others, credit dreams as an important source of creative inspiration. The tune for Paul McCartney's song 'Yesterday' (possibly the most frequently played song of all time), came directly from a dream! Where does this inspiration come from? I believe it's the angels themselves!

Have you ever heard the phrase 'Why don't you sleep on it?' with reference to a problem? Now you know why!

ANGEL NAMES

Angels don't really need names but it is human to name things. Many people feel more comfortable giving their own angels a name, and the angels are quite happy about this.

Some angels work with modern-day names like Angela or James, whereas others seem to fit a more 'traditional-sounding' angel name like Taramiel or Joshuel. Angels don't seem to mind what they are called; they are just happy to be recognized and acknowledged.

There are many ways to find your angel's name:

♥ You can just pick a name which 'sounds right', and call your angel that.

♥ Sit in quiet meditation or contemplation and ask for a name to be given you – take the first name that comes to you.

♥ Write down your request before you go to sleep at night. Your angel name may appear as part of a dream or vision, or you may wake up in the morning with the name in your mind.

♥ Or try the angel meditation exercise on page 245.

What if you don't like the name you receive? Remember that angels do not mind what they are called! Change it to something that feels right to you.

ANGEL NOTES

Make the angel your symbol. You can use it on letterheads and notecards for friends and relations. Try making your own stationery. You don't have to be a great artist – a simple sketch will work. Alternatively, work on an angel image and when you are happy with it scan it into a computer (or ask someone else to) and add your own personal touch to the top of your letterheads.

Keeping in contact with people can be hard work. In our modern life we are always busy and following the tradition of letter writing can be difficult to keep up. Not everyone has access to computers (or would be able to use one even if they did) and there is nothing nicer and more individual than a personal letter arriving on your doormat.

Use your angel stationery to keep up-to-date with friends and relations. If you are short of time, send a notebook with angel sayings or quotes inside. Your thoughts will be much appreciated. Check out postcards with angel statues and angel figures in cities with beautiful churches or lovely paintings. Buy a selection and keep them in stock with the stamps already stuck on. Make keeping-in-touch easy.

Don't forget to use your notes for people who live closer, too. An angel note on top of a pillow or slipped into a pocket or bag will remind people that you care.

ANGEL PHOTOGRAPHS

Do you have images of loved ones lying around in a drawer? You can buy or make your own angel frames to put them in. Make a visual request to literally 'surround your friends and relations with angels', asking your angels to protect and take care of them for you.

- ♥ Use frames that already have angel images and figures around the outside.

- ♥ Use plain frames and paint or draw images of angels around the frame.

- ♥ Cut out images of angels from wrapping paper and paste them around the edge. When it's dry, protect with a layer of spray varnish.

- ♥ Lay the image of your loves ones – or several together – on a piece of light card. Glue the images down. Surround the edges with angels and frame the whole thing under glass.

- ♥ Add a special saying to the frame such as 'Aunty Mary – protected by angels', or your favourite angel saying or quote.

If you prefer your photographs in books, mount your photographs on light card as above, surround them with images of angels and then slide them into ordinary plastic-sleeved angel photograph albums.

ANGEL POETRY

Angels are creative beings who inspire many people to write. Following the notes suggested for writing with your angels, request that your angels express themselves through poetry with you.

At first your words may seem awkward and disjointed. As with all angel work, practice makes perfect and you only need to 'want' to do this to be able to learn. Select a special angel notebook to record your musings.

ANGEL PRAYERS

Prayers are like music of love to angels. It is right to pray to and with the angels, as they are directly linked with the source (or God-essence). Angels often need our requests to work with us efficiently. They long for us to ask for their help.

How do you pray to an angel? Any way you want! Traditionally you might get down on your knees and pray. You can ask for help and also take the opportunity to say thank you for your blessings. We all have many blessings in our lives, even when we are not aware of them or appreciate them all the time.

How about making a list of your blessings? What could you thank the angels for in your life? The love of your family and friends? Do you always get a smile from your neighbour or a friendly word from the lady at the post office? The home in which you live? Do you have somewhere safe to sleep at night or a dry place to eat? How about the animals in your life? Do you own fish, or cats? Do you ride horses or feed the birds each day? Do you enjoy watching the antics of squirrels or seeing sheep graze in the fields?

Maybe you have other things that mean a lot to you. These things can be material objects which bring you joy. It is OK to enjoy the abundance which the angels can help us to achieve. Remember to be thankful in your angel prayers. The angels can take your messages right to God.

Your prayers go something like this:

'Angels, I thank you for your help. I appreciated your closeness when Sandra was ill and I am thankful for your comfort when Billy had to go to the vet. I enjoyed it so much when Dad managed a smile today and I loved it when Jacob was finally able to take off his plastercast. Thank you for helping me with my garden. I love the new car and I am grateful for all of your support and protection over my family each day.'

Your prayers can be very personal to you and you can use the words which feel right and fit your own life. After you have finished your prayers you can end with the words 'thank you', or with a phrase which fits your religious beliefs. Remember that angels are not about religion but about love. So use your prayers as a way of asking for help and counting your blessings.

You can say your prayers when you are alone or pray with a group of people. You may wish to pray after every meal or every morning and evening. Your way is the right way for you.

If you feel inspired you can just make something up as you go along or, if your prefer, write down your prayers. Write them in your journal, or cut them out and stick them into your scrapbook!

Make Your Own Angel Prayer Cards

The archangels each have special roles and tasks. You can make your own angel prayer cards by taking the attributes of each angel and creating a prayer to each in turn. Every card can have a phrase of praise in honour of the archangel, to address them and request their particular talents and abilities into your life.

Your phrase might be something like this:

'Archangel Michael, I send you blessings and thank you for your loving protection. I ask your help with caring for my children whilst I am at work, and thank you for your guidance. Amen.'

You can make your prayer card for a specific purpose. Decorate it and place it where you can see it on a regular basis.

'Archangel Gabriel, God's holy messenger, I would like to request your loving assistance in sending positive thoughts to my son [add name here] who is currently serving in the army and is out of family contact. I ask this in God's love. Amen.'

This would work well with the words actually written on the back of a photograph of the person. As with all of these ideas, the cards act as another 'point of focus', which gives more energy to your request.

A lot of studies are currently being carried out on the power of prayer. Blind studies (which include two groups: one group of people who were prayed for and another that were not) have proved that the group who received the positive prayer work were healed more successfully than those who did not. Prayer works. Prayer, like music, is often called the voice of the angels.

ANGEL SCRAPBOOKS

Angel scrapbooks are a little like angel journals – but with pictures and cuttings! If you want, your angel journal can 'be' a scrapbook as well, but you will probably want to keep that a little neater.

You can buy a book specifically for the purpose or make your own by stapling together large stiff paper of different colours. If you are a crafty person you may already have discovered websites and craft shops that supply stickers, special shaped scissors and other odds-and-ends for prettying up your book.

What can you stick in your scrapbook?

♥ Poems you've copied or written yourself. Anything that inspires you. Write or type them out on pretty paper and then mount them in your book. Decorate with images around the edges.

♥ Cut out phrases or notes from magazines and newspapers which you find uplifting.

♥ Angel stories – your own or others.

♥ Postcards with angel figures from museums and galleries from around the world. How about asking people to post them to you?

♥ Miraculous life-saving stories.

♥ Beautiful images from Christmas cards

♥ Photographs of breathtaking views of special places which have made you feel 'close to the angels'.

♥ Photographs of people who have changed your life.

♥ Letters from special 'earth angel' friends.

♥ Pressed flowers from riverbanks or hill walks where you have felt your angels with you.

Making an angel scrapbook is a way of recording your blissful moments. It's about reminding yourself that life is special and that every day is a miracle. Often those moments will be recreated in your mind when you create your book.

When you are feeling low, open your angel scrapbook and remember those special times.

～◯

Communicating with angels is about having fun and connecting with love. Angels are around us all the time just waiting for the word. They long to inspire us. Be inspired!

Contacting the Author

Jacky welcomes letters and emails from readers about their own angel stories and paranormal experiences.

You can contact her via the publishers:

Jacky Newcomb
c/o Element
HarperCollins Publishers Ltd
77–85 Fulham Palace Road
London W6 8JB

or you can visit Jacky at her personal website:

www.angellady.co.uk

Index